T0228586

The Ultimate Guide
to Snapchat

Turner Publishing Company
Nashville, Tennessee
www.turnerpublishing.com

The Ultimate Guide to Snapchat

Cover and book design by Archie Ferguson

Library of Congress Control Number: 2021946555

9781684428274 paperback
9781684428281 hardcover
9781684428298 ebook

Printed in the United States of America

The Ultimate Guide to Snapchat

PHIL WALTON
Official Lens Creator for Snapchat

TURNER
PUBLISHING COMPANY

The Ultimate Guide
to Snapchat

TABLE OF CONTENTS

INTRODUCTION

It's easy to see the cultural impact that Snapchat has had on our lives on the Internet. They've redefined the word "filter" to mean something that adds to our world instead of taking something away. Through constant innovation, Snapchat has continued to grow its user base and maintain its relevance to an entire generation.

As Snap celebrates its tenth year—which is no small feat in the volatile tech industry—I'm proud to create this guide to help more people understand and use this application in their own digital social life. The good people at Snap actually helped me with the research for this book, and while it isn't an official guide, I'm confident that the information here will be accurate and relevant to you. Whether you're entirely new to the application or looking for some hidden secrets, there should be a little something for everyone.

It may be hard to believe, but I consider myself a relative newcomer to Snapchat. I was one generation back from the kids who grew up with smartphones and had Snapchat as their primary means of communication. There was a learning curve when I first tried it out. Snapchat is an app that encourages you to explore and discover—and there is a lot there to get into. But sometimes it's nice to have a guide that shows you where everything is. I honestly learned a few new things myself as I researched. My goal is that by the end of this book, you'll be able to use Snapchat like a seasoned pro.

Maybe you're still trying to decide why you should be using Snapchat or whether you're going to allow your teenager to use it. I've spoken with a few people who either don't have Snapchat or downloaded it but never use it. I hope to change that. Snapchat has so many amazing features that can enrich the way you communicate with your friends, family, and the world. It may not replace your other social media channels, but it could easily become your favorite.

Some great features:

- Chat—Send disappearing text or video messages without using up phone memory
- Filters/Lenses—The best way to augment your reality
- Stories—Catch up on everyday candid moments of your friends and celebrities
- Discover—Snap Originals and branded content that's interesting to you
- Games and Minis—Quickly drop into a game with your friends, wherever you are
- . . . and so many more things I'm excited to share!

I'm glad you've chosen to join me. Get ready to expand your horizons with Snapchat!

HOW I FELL IN LOVE WITH SNAPCHAT

It was not long after Snapchat rewarded me with my verification star that I did a silly thing: I started a cult. On Snapchat.

Now, I can imagine that this provocative statement has whacked an entire bees' nest of questions for you, and let me first set your mind at ease. No, it wasn't a real cult. No one got hurt, brainwashed, or exploited in any way. It was really a small online community centered around my Snapchat Lens work. The whole "cult" name was really just an edgy nomenclature—possibly because "The Mickey Mouse Club" was already taken. Who knows? So allow me to explain how it went down.

I had been a part of the Official Lens Creators (OLC) program—a program Snapchat designed to reward creators who were engaging Snapchatters with viral, original AR content on the platform or helping other Lens Creators on their forum—and had made quite a few Lenses, but I wasn't one of the superstars like CyreneQ, Paper Triangles, or Jinnie the Wew. My most popular Lens at the time was Rainbow Unicorn.

Scan the Snapcode here
(open Snapchat to the main camera screen
and press on the image to unlock)
if you want to try it.

This Lens had around a million views at the time, which is good, but many of my other Lenses had mere thousands or tens of thousands, if that. As a digital artist, I was looking for a way to reach a bigger audience for my work. I only had a handful of friends on Snapchat, so I didn't have a lot of people that I could share my creations with. But after I was verified (which simply means that Snapchat recognized me as an official account, similar to the blue checks of Twitter/Instagram), I noticed that people suddenly began to subscribe to me on Snapchat. This was some new attention that I'd never received before. These subscribers were people who liked my Lens creations and wanted to see more of my stuff! It was just a few at first, but that number was growing. After I talked to a social media influencer who was much savvier than myself, he suggested that I start posting to my public Snapchat story.

My first thought was that no one in their right mind would care about what I would post. I'm both too boring and too private to hang my whole life out there like some kind of Jenner/Kardashian. But perhaps a few insomniacs might find my musings to be a natural sleep aid. Plus, I could at a minimum let my subscribers know when I made a new Snapchat Lens. That alone would be worth it.

So I began posting things from my life. I promised my wife early on, for privacy reasons, that I would never put up a picture of her or my daughters—which is a good rule, I think. But our cats and dog were pretty photogenic, so therefore fair game.

Then I found a third-party app called Sendit that integrates with Snapchat and allowed me to ask for questions from my fans, which I could then answer. This was a game changer for me. I soon had people from all over the world asking me questions on any number of topics. And what with my being a father, I was already well-versed in sounding like I know what I'm talking about.

And the questions didn't stop, either. I'd answer one and get five more. My entire message queue would fill in a day. I couldn't keep up. And the people sending questions sometimes had follow-ups. But because the questions were anonymous, my fans began to include names with their questions. They were self-chosen made-up names at first, but then people began asking me to make up a name for them. This became so popular that, for a while, that was all I was being asked.

I jokingly referred to this impromptu community as a cult—in reference to the seemingly fanatical devotion of the followers and the fact that I was now renaming everyone. Not long after,the "cult" became known as The Philluminati. Fan art was made. Some very industrious followers created an entire Discord server for it. And for a season it was a whole big thing. I eventually ran out of steam trying to come up with original names for every single person who came along, so I even created a special Snapchat name randomizer Lens to do just that for me. Want to find out your Philluminati Name?

Try it here:

Snapchat enabled me to communicate and connect with people around the world—people I probably never would have had the opportunity to speak with. And that's pretty special, as far as I'm concerned. So, to make a long story longer, this is why I fell in love with Snapchat and why I still use it every day.

If you haven't already, go to the Search bar on Snapchat, type in my username (@phillip.walton), and subscribe. I promise wholesome content, and you'll not only get first notice of the latest Lens that I've created, but also a good chance to see one of my cats or my dog . . . possibly even a duck. Who knows?

A BRIEF HISTORY OF SNAPCHAT

Snapchat was built by Evan Spiegel and Bobby Murphy (who met at Stanford), launching in the App Store in September 2011. The idea for Snapchat, pioneered by Spiegel, Murphy, and another man named Reggie Brown, was for people to share real human moments with each other—not glamorized color-corrected selfies or food pictures with heavy photo editing. As it turned out, people liked a platform where they could be real with each other. And with disappearing messages, the feel was more like an ongoing conversation than a court reporter's record of evidence. The appeal to young people was clear, and Snapchat quickly grew in popularity, adding millions of daily active users to become the social media powerhouse it is today. At the time of writing, Snapchat has 265 million daily active users who create over 5 billion Snaps every single day. Over 75 percent of 13- to 34-year-olds in the United States use Snapchat—with similar statistics for users in Germany, England, France, and Australia.

WHAT CAN SNAPCHAT DO FOR YOU?

There's quite a bit of depth to Snapchat and a lot you can do with it, but essentially Snapchat is about sharing moments with other people. Snapchat is a tool to help you stay connected with friends, family, influencers, and your audience/customers. The camera tools allow you to take and share videos and pictures, either directly with your friends or through your story where people can see them at their leisure. The chat function lets you message people instantly with text, audio, photos, or video—or even make calls to other Snapchat users. And you can also check out the various kinds of content on the platform as well—everything from augmented reality experiences to fully produced professional shows formatted for your phone screen.

Whether you're someone interested in connecting with friends who already use Snapchat, a parent who is keeping tabs on your teen's social media activity, or a brand manager using Snapchat to communicate with your audience or customers, Snapchat's feature-rich environment gives you many possibilities. How you make the most of it is up to you.

Now that we've covered a few background topics, it's time to get into using Snapchat. The first step is to have the Snapchat app installed on your smartphone. You can download it from either the Apple App Store for iOS or from Google Play if you have an Android device.

Once the app is installed, open it, and you will be prompted to sign up for an account. Don't forget to review the terms and conditions. It's important to note that while Snap does try to keep the content on their platform safe for everyone to enjoy, Snapchat accounts are not for children under thirteen.

When signing up, Snapchat will ask for your birthday, a username, a strong password (at least 8 characters), and a phone number. For more information on setting up your password, see page 78. Snapchat will also require access to your phone's camera, microphone, and photo library. Once you do that, you'll be ready to go.

General Info: *Usernames*

Consider carefully what you want for a username—it will be yours for the long haul and is nearly impossible to change. Think of your Snapchat username as being like a professional email adress. I recommend a firstname.lastname convention if that's available. Friends I've known who picked a username that's weird, offensive, or difficult to remember end up regretting it.

ADDING FRIENDS

Now that you've entered your own information, let's add the "social" to our social network. Allow Snapchat access to your Contacts and it will provide you with a list of friends who are already on the platform. Find the people you want to connect with and hit the + Add button to send them a friend request. Snap's built-in privacy and safety features require your connection to be mutual, so they will have to accept your request before you're fully connected. You may also find that some of your friends who already have Snapchat have sent you requests. You'll see them on the Add Friends screen under the section "Added Me." All you need to do is hit the + Accept button and you'll be connected.

YOUR BITMOJI

One final thing that everyone should do to fully maximize their Snapchat experience is to set up their Bitmoji. A Bitmoji is a little cartoon avatar of you that is used throughout Snapchat—in stickers, filters, games, minis, Bitmoji stories, and even in some custom Snapchat Lenses.

To get started, download the Bitmoji app from the iOS App Store or Google Play, then link it to your Snapchat account. The Bitmoji app will walk you through the setup process to get your Bitmoji looking great—and remember, even though your Bitmoji is your avatar, you can change it to look however you want. There's constantly new updates for clothing styles as well, so you'll never run out of options. My own personal Bitmoji dresses better than I do.

Once your avatar is set up in the Bitmoji app, you'll need to activate it in Snapchat as well so that Snap has permission to use it. Tap your profile icon and then Add Bitmoji; the app will guide you through the rest. Once it's linked, you can also edit your Bitmoji and change its outfit style on the Bitmoji app, or inside Snapchat from the profile menu. One cool thing about Bitmojis is that they are available outside Snapchat. Some apps like Venmo have direct integration with Bitmoji; others will let you access the Bitmoji keyboard (after activating it in your device keyboard settings first). There's even a Chrome extension for Bitmojis, so you can easily drop them in an email or Google Doc.

Once your account is set up, you're signed in, and have added a few friends, you're ready to explore the world of Snapchat. Let's familiarize ourselves with Snapchat's interface.

General Info: *Snapchat Software*

Snapchat is an app that is in active development. With that, some features may change or get removed without warning. They also roll out different features at different times and to different regions. Snap also uses A-B testing with their software, which means sometimes people in the "A" group have features that the "B" group people don't—or vice versa. All that is to say, the following screens/menus are accurate to what most Snapchat users in general have—but may be different from what you specifically have.

When you first open Snapchat, it defaults to the main screen. Each section of the User Interface is labeled below.

A. Record Button
B. Pre-Snap Creative Tools
C. Post-Snap Creative Tools
D. Action Bar
E. Profile/Settings
F. Search
G. Add Friends
H. Memories
I. Lens Carousel

Record Button

Tap to take a photo Snap or hold the button down to record a video, and release to stop the recording. As you're recording, a yellow ring will begin to form around the button, which indicates the length of your video. Also, if you're recording a video, you can slide left to the "lock" symbol while recording to keep the recording going even if you aren't holding your finger on the button. If you record a video for over ten seconds, you will have the option to trim it.

Pre-Snap Creative Tools

Change camera settings before you take a Snap. Flip from front to back camera, or change flash settings, Timeline, Sounds, Multi Snap, Timer, Focus, or Grid. The chapter on Pre-Snap Creative Tools will explain what each of these is in greater detail.

Post-Snap Creative Tools

Add additional creative elements after you've taken a Snap: Text, Drawing, Stickers, Scissors (cut out your own sticker), Sounds, Attach Link, Crop, and Timer. I'll break down each of these in the Post-Snap Creative Tools chapter.

ACTION BAR

The main navigation bar of Snapchat. Each button takes you to its own screen with tons of features. We'll explore each one in greater detail in the coming chapters. But for now, here's a quick overview:

Snap Map

Displays your location on a map if you've given Snapchat permission for that information. If your friends have done the same, you'll see their location on the map as well, shown from the last place they opened up Snapchat and had Internet access. The map also shows the area name and local temperature. You can also see a heat map of where local Snaps are being created and published to "Our Story."

Chat

The area for sending messages and Snaps directly to friends or groups of friends. In the chat screen, you can also play live multiplayer games and minis.

Hidden Feature: *Quick Navigation*

You don't need to use the action bar to get around inside Snapchat. Depending on which screen you're on, you can swipe left, right, up, or down to find the other screens.

Scan

A very recent change to Snap's interface is when you are on the Camera screen, the Camera button changes to a Scan button, making it that much easier to access the screen scanning function. To learn more about this incredible feature, jump to the chapter on Lenses.

Stories and Discover

Here is where you can view 24-hour stories made by your friends and celebrities you subscribed to. In the Discover section, there is short-form entertainment and news formatted for your Snapchat screen.

Spotlight

Similar to TikTok's main page, Spotlight features popular and top user-submitted Snaps of the day.

PROFILE/SETTINGS

Access your account information, set up a public profile, edit your Bitmoji, edit account settings, and even see insights on your story. You can also add friends and see who you Snap the most.

Search

Find friends, discover shows and cool new Lenses.

Add Friends

When someone adds you as a friend, you'll get a notification. Once you add them back, you're then linked and can share Snaps and conversations.

Memories

Here is the archive of your saved Snaps, Stories, camera roll, and My Eyes Only (private) Snaps. Here in Memories, your Snaps are organized by date. And at the beginning of each month, Snapchat automatically creates a re-cap—which gives you a fun highlight reel of your Snaps from the previous month. Remember that Snaps posted to your friends, or your story aren't automatically saved, unless you change your settings, so the way to keep that awesome Snap you just created is to hit that Save button.

General Info: *My Eyes Only*

Worth a brief mention, the My Eyes Only section is for Snaps that you want to keep extra-private. It will require an extra passcode (or passphrase) to access these Snaps. To save a Snap to My Eyes Only, tap the Check button while in Memories and select the Snaps you want to move to My Eyes Only, and then tap the More button at the bottom to find the option for Hide Snap. Remember that My Eyes Only Snaps stay private only while they're in this section—if you post them or send them to another person, it's possible for your private Snap to get screenshotted and shared at that point.

Lens Carousel

Tap this button to bring up the Snapchat Lens Carousel and the menu for additional Lens possibilities. Here you'll find a curated list of Lenses and Snappable games from Snapchat. Check out the chapter on Lenses for lots more information about the Carousel, Lenses, and other incredible augmented-reality features.

Now that you have general knowledge of the main functions of Snapchat, let's dive right in and teach you how to start making your own Snaps. The basic user-experience flow is to record your Snap with the camera and tools, then either send it to a friend or post it to your Snap story. The process goes like this:

I. Take a picture or video using the Record button.
2. Tap the yellow "Send To" button in the bottom right corner to bring up your contact list.
3. Select the destination(s) for your Snap to be sent to—you can choose more than one. Destinations will be displayed at the bottom of the screen in blue.
4. Hit the white button with the blue arrow at the bottom right screen to post your Snap.

That's it! Try it out. Send a smiling selfie to a friend in your contact list. Don't worry about doing anything too fancy at the moment, just get familiar with the process. This is a direct Snap between you and someone else. You can also send a direct Snap to more than one person, just by tapping on their names in your contact list.

So let's say you've got an awesome-looking Snap, and you want everyone to see it. You could send it out to your entire contact list, but there's a better way to do it. If you want your Snap to stick around a bit longer (24 hours) in a place where friends and followers can view it at their convenience, that's called a Story.

WHAT'S A STORY?

After taking a Snap, you have to tell Snapchat which story you want it to go to. And you'll have a few different options from which to choose for where that is. Stories are a built-in privacy feature, which leaves the decision up to you about who sees your Snaps. Trust me, as someone who once naïvely posted a public Snap that had my feet in it, things got bizarre. The Internet gets so weird about feet, and I should have just kept that among friends. Here's what each of the stories are and who can see them.

My Story

Private to your friends only. Which means only people you've already friended can see this story.

Snap Map

Snaps posted here are viewable by the public and appear as part of the "heat map" for Snaps in a geographic region. Anyone browsing the Snap Map may be able to see your post if they tap on that region.

New Group/Private Story

Got a close group of friends you want to share Snaps with? You can create a private story so your Snaps are only seen by that group of friends, or create a Private Group story that all the members of that group can post to. This is a much better place to post that foot pic, if you're into that kind of thing.

Spotlight

Snap's content-discovery page is similar to TikTok. Post your best video Snaps (with audio) here for a chance to win part of the large cash reward they give out daily to top Spotlight creators.

Public Story

If you're over 18, you have the option to set up your public profile, where you can post your Snaps to a story seen by your subscribers and beyond. It's possible for your public story to even appear in Snapchat's Discovery section as recommended content for certain users—which could mean a lot of eyeballs on your Snaps. For those of you who are interested in developing an audience, whether you're an influencer or brand, or maybe just someone who wants to share something unique with the world, your public profile is the place to begin.

USING SNAPCHAT FILTERS

There's a bit of confusion over the difference between a Snapchat Lens and a filter. Basically, a filter is just an image overlay on top of your Snap, while a Lens is an actual augmented reality experience. Both are great for quickly adding some visual interest to your Snap. Lenses are accessible from the Lens Carousel or Lens Explorer and must be activated before you take a Snap. But how do you activate a filter? It's easy.

Once you've taken a Snap, either a photo or video, swipe left or right to activate a filter. Snapchat has several color-changing (or LUT, if you prefer) filters to change the image color to warm tones, old film, or even black-and-white. You'll also find overlay stickers, filters that appear contextually depending on time of day and your location. On a Monday morning, you'll get messages like "Need Coffee" or "New Day, Let's Get it!" or Saturday afternoon you may see "Chill Vibes" or "Relaxing Weekend." You'll also find location-based filters on the city you're in if you allow access for Snap to see your location. You'll find a filter for the Arch in St. Louis or the Space Needle in Seattle. Context-sensitive filters can also display your name, time of day, and even local temperature. Snapchat also includes advertisement filters as well that are sponsored by brands. If you've created a video Snap, you will also find time-manipulation filters that can slow down, speed up, or play your footage in reverse.

Bonus Feature: *Stacking Effects*

Did you know you can stack up to three filters by hitting the +Layers button to add a new filter on top of your existing one?

It's also possible to create your own custom filters for a particular location at a specific time. These are perfect for events like wedding receptions or birthday parties. There are free options if you make them yourself, or an online creator tool that does cost money to create, depending on the time and the size of the area where you want your filter to be available. Learn more in the Geofilters section, or make your own at Snapchat.com/create.

Using Snapchat Lenses

And finally, we'd be remiss if we didn't create a Snap using one of the millions of awesome augmented reality Lenses available. There's no single description for what you'll find in a Snapchat Lens. Some are as simple as changing the colors on-screen, or smoothing out your skin and whitening your teeth. Some are elaborate 3D environmental experiences that you can walk around inside.

So on the main camera screen, tap anywhere in the main area to bring up the Lens Carousel. Swipe through the different Lens options in the Carousel to try out a few.

Please note that the Lenses in the Carousel are not the same for every user. They're also updated daily, so you may find something you like one day that's gone the next. Fortunately, there are ways to find your favorites again. With the Lens active, an information button appears in the upper left part of the screen, just below your profile image. Tap on it to bring up more information about the Lens. A pop-up will list the Lens's name and creator's name. To the right of that is a gray heart button. Tap that to add this Lens to your favorites. You can also tap "Copy Lens Link" in the menu below. That will give you a direct link to that Lens (Community Lenses only). This is very useful if you found a fun Lens in Snapchat and want to use it with Snap Camera—the desktop virtual camera software that lets you use Lenses with your webcam. We'll discuss Snap Camera in further detail later in the book.

But instead of selecting one of the Carousel Lenses, let's search for one Lens in particular. Tap the search icon at the top and type in "Potato." With any luck, the search results will return one potato Lens in particular. Tap on Potato by Phil Walton, and soon you will be experiencing the world-famous tuber that is my own claim to fame. If you're up for it, record a short video saying hello to me and everyone reading this book using the potato Lens, then hit Send To and check Spotlight—don't forget to add the #snapchatbook hashtag under Topics before you submit. Later on in the Search section, I'll show you a trick where you can see everyone's Snaps, including yours, using it.

You did it! You're Snapping like a pro. But we've only begun to scratch the surface of what's possible with Snapchat, so let's dig a little deeper.

Taking Good Snaps

Due to the fast-paced and "consumable" nature of social media, it can be tempting to overlook quality as you create Snaps. I think this is a mistake. The cameras built in to our phones boast amazing specs, capable of high-resolution, low-light, high-speed, slow-motion, and computer-enhanced imagery to make us (and the world around us) look our best. So why would it make sense to use that kind of camera to take poor photos or videos? A Snap, after all, is an extension of the camera's functionality. Why not use the tools at your disposal to create striking images? Sure, there will be times when you want to quickly capture a unique, silly, or amazing moment—and there's no time to worry about the principles of photography; but most of the time, with just a tiny bit of thought and planning, we can take better Snaps that people will be excited to see.

Much of what makes a good Snap comes down to the principles of good photography. There are entire degree programs at colleges and universities that can teach this in much better depth than I can in this short chapter, but here are just a few elements to consider as you're taking pictures (and video) with Snapchat.

For Still-Camera Photography

Subject: What are you photographing? Why is it interesting? See if you can make your Snap capture the essence of what you see in your subject.

Frame: What is around your subject? Make sure you're capturing only what's important. Don't forget that Snapchat's camera uses a portrait/vertical frame. Pay attention to what's happening above and below your subject as well.

Lighting: Lighting is incredible for setting a mood in an image. Bright and sunny means something very different from dark and long shadows. Consider the lighting of your scene and make sure it reflects the mood of your Snap. Note that lighting that's too dim, though, will create a Snap where no one can see what's going on at all.

Color: Similar to lighting, color can also communicate mood.

Rule of Thirds: If you divide the screen into thirds both horizontally and vertically, the four points where these intersect are the strongest points of interest on-screen. Placing your subject at one of these points makes for a more aesthetically pleasing image. Snapchat even has a quick screen guide to help you figure out where these points are—just tap the frame button.

Distance: How close or far away you are from your subject can also change how you feel about it. A subject that's very close to the camera can feel intimate or perhaps claustrophobic. On the other hand, the effect of a subject's being far away can be to make the subject feel epic in scale or even isolated.

Focus: Most cameras come with aggressive autofocus functions that will try to get as much of your image in focus as possible. But there are times when it's nice to have a soft focus on either the foreground or background.

Quick tip: *Focus Point*

You can easily change the point of focus when using Snapchat. Just tap the screen where you want the camera to focus.

For Video

In addition to applying the rules of good photography, there are a few extra considerations when you are shooting video Snaps.

Time: There's a common wisdom in film editing that says "each cut should be only as long as it needs to be." It's a good thing to keep in mind as you shoot video Snaps. People have short attention spans and will skip a video where nothing seems to be happening. But on the other side of that, we also need a moment to orient ourselves when watching a video—to understand the scene and what we're about to see. Video clips that go by too quickly for us to understand just leave us confused.

Camera Movement: Many people's complaints about "Found footage" movies is that oftentimes the camera is moving around so much that we can't even see what's going on. For some people it even makes them nauseated. Consider how smoothly you're holding your phone as you shoot video with Snapchat. Smooth, even movements definitely make for a better viewing experience.

PRE-SNAP

Even before you take a picture or video, you have some great tools at your disposal to help you create that great Snap. Let's examine them and see what they can do to help.

Flip Camera

A standard feature for any camera app. This allows you to switch between the front- and back-facing cameras. The front camera is great for taking selfies and using Snapchat Lenses that utilize face tracking. The back camera on your phone is typically of higher resolution, using multiple Lenses for creating better images.

General Info: *LIDAR*

At the time of writing, some of the newest smartphones have just added LiDAR technology to the back camera—which gives your device an understanding of depth in the scene. Why is this cool? Traditionally cameras view the world as a flat image—like a photograph. But with LiDAR, your phone views the world more like we do with our own eyes, a 3D understanding with depth that allows it to understand which objects are in front of another or how far back something is. With Snapchat's LiDAR-enabled Lenses, you can do amazing things like see computer-generated flowers grow out of your desktop or have hundreds of butterflies along the walls of your room.

Flash

Another standard feature for camera apps. The flash can be useful for brightening up a dark environment when you take a picture or video. I'm personally of the opinion that flash adds harsh light and doesn't make for good images, so I keep this feature disabled most of the time, using it only when I absolutely need it because the ambient light is totally insufficient.

Timeline

This feature lets you create a TikTok-style multiple-video-clip edit for your Snap. When you hit the Timeline button, you'll see a little shaded bar appear below the Record button. As you record your video, you'll see that bar start to fill up with your clips, represented by yellow dashes. The Redo button will discard your last clip so you can rerecord it if you want. Then hitting the yellow check button will assemble your timeline into one Snap that you can post or send to your friends. You also have the option to add a sound clip as well.

Sounds

This adds a sound clip or music to your Snap. Hitting this button brings up Snapchat's collection of licensed music clips. Use the search bar to find the particular song you're looking for, or scroll through to discover something new. You can also tap the "My Sounds" tab and record your own. Preview the sound with the Play button. Tap on the song name to add it to your Snap—even if you haven't recorded anything yet.

You have the option to attach the sound after you've recorded your Snap; but if you add sound first, you can hear it play as you record your video, which is helpful if you're trying to lip-sync or make your actions correspond to the music.

> ### Hidden Feature: *Sound-Clip Edit*
>
> With a sound clip attached to your Snap, you can drag along the clip to select the portion of it that you want to use. Maybe you don't want to start at the very beginning of the clip, or maybe you just want to catch the chorus. Drag the scrubber to where you want it, and a time indicator will appear to show how far into the clip you are. Hit Play to preview. Then all you have to do is take your Snap, and the sound will play from the perfect spot.

Multi Snap

String a series of individual Snaps together. This is very similar to the Timeline tool, with a key difference—it puts multiple Snaps in a sequence and allows you to edit each one. With the Multi Snap button selected, you'll see a plus sign appear at the center of the record button. After you record a series of Snaps and hit the "Edit and Send" button, you can edit each Snap individually. Trim the duration of the video, add stickers, and use the other Post-Snap Creative tools. You can even delete a Snap in the sequence that you don't want. Once you're finished, you can post the entire series to your story or send it to friends. Be aware that once you hit the "Edit and Send" button, you can no longer add any additional clips. And canceling out of it will lose all of your clips in the Multi Snap. Note that the clips to create with Multi Snap will post to your story as individual Snaps—as opposed to Time-line, which builds your clips into one Snap.

Timer

The timer is useful if you want to take a photo or video but can't be there to tap the record button. When selected, the timer gives you a 3-second count-down before taking a picture or recording a video for up to 10 seconds. The button defaults to a photo snap; but if you tap the timer a second time, you can set the length of recording for a video Snap.

Focus

Perfect for the front-facing camera, the Focus tool adds a soft blur to the background behind you. It gives you that "portrait studio" look without head-ing down to the Glamour Shots at the mall.

3D

This mode is only available on the front camera and only on newer cam-eras that have two lenses on the front side. 3D mode takes a picture with both cameras and combines them with some post-processing to simulate a three-dimensional version of the image. The Snap will automatically have a soft background blur and rotate slightly to show the 3D effect. You can even tilt your phone around to control the effect yourself.

Hidden Feature: *3D Filters*

Snap has also created special 3D filters that work specifically with this tool. After taking a Snap with the 3D tool, swipe left or right to access them.

Grid

If you remember back in the previous section about Taking Good Snaps, where I talked about the Rule of Thirds, you'll understand why the grid is useful. With the grid selected, it divides your screen into nine boxes—or into thirds horizontally and vertically. There's also a level center function that tells you if you're holding your camera perpendicular to the ground. These grid guides allow you to easily compose your image into something a little more aesthetically pleasing—even if it is just a picture of your bad hair day or your dog being a total derp.

Pre-Snap Tools Summary

The Pre-Snap tools offer you some solid options for creating more interesting Snaps. As the name suggests, these tools are there to help you plan or put a little forethought into your Snap before you create it. Most of the time when you take a photo or video, you will probably not be thinking about composition, timing, or the use of light and color. But the very act of taking a Snap and sending it out into the world is a creative act of communication. And without trying to sound too high-minded, doesn't effective communication improve our relationships and therefore our lives?

I'm not suggesting that the selfie you post to Snapchat will immediately make your life better; but your Snap could make a friend smile or offer some encouragement, so maybe in fact it could.

For those of you who are looking to go beyond the random, sporadic postings that most people do on social media, Pre-Snap tools like the Timeline and Multi Snap offer the possibility of building a narrative as you post. This is what pioneering Russian film theorist and director Sergei Eisenstein called Montage theory. With Images (or video clips) placed together, our brains want to connect them with meaning, thus giving you the opportunity to connect your Snaps together to tell a story. Really, that can be something as simple as before and after, setup and punchline, or beginning, middle, and end. For those following your story, a narrative arc is far more interesting than occasional disjointed images and videos from your life. Planning out what you're going to shoot and then strategically using the creative tools (including Lenses) will help create stronger, more loyal audience engagement.

POST-SNAP

After you've taken your Snap, the toolbar on the right changes to give you more creative options to enhance your Snap. Let's take a look at each one.

Text

Adds a block of text to your Snap, with multiple styles and colors to choose from. Tap the T button to start a text block. While in Edit mode, you can swipe on the "Styles" bar (located just above the keyboard) to change your font style. Use the color slider to change the font (or background) color. Use the justify button at top to align the text block Left, Center, or Right. Change your font size with the pinch zoom functionality. Once you've got your text saying the right thing, tap elsewhere on the screen and now you can place, rotate, or resize that block of text. Remember aesthetics when you're placing text and choosing color. Dark text against a dark background is usually unreadable. Phone screens come in different sizes, so text placed in the "trim area" at the top or bottom of the screen could get cut off on different devices. And also don't forget to proofread your text before you send it off. Not just for spelling/grammar errors, either. I've sent out more than a few Snaps that have an entire word either wrong or missing. Once that Snap is posted or sent, you can't edit it anymore—only delete it and start over.

General Info: *Text Blocks*

While there is a character limit if you're writing an essay, you can just add another (and another) block of text and complete your important thoughts. The "Classic" text block is the only one that will not allow you to scale and rotate the text on screen.

@ tagging

The coolest part of the text block is that you can tag another Snapchat user. Just hit the @ symbol, and Snapchat will automatically bring up a short list of friends that you've recently exchanged Snaps with; or you can start typing their name or username in your Snap. When you post that Snap to your story, it will automatically send it out to your tagged friend(s) as well. This is great if you're taking a group picture with a bunch of friends and want them all to see it. Or if you take a Snap that you think one of your friends in particular might enjoy and you don't want them to miss it.

Hidden Feature: *Deleting Elements*

What if you make a block of text, or place a sticker in your Snap, but you don't want it anymore? Just press and hold on the object, until it activates drag mode, then drag the item to the bottom middle of your screen, where a trash icon will appear. Release, and it's gone. But be careful: sometimes you could be trying to actually place an item in that area and it gets accidentally deleted.

Doodle

Feel like flexing your awesome drawing skills? The doodle tool is perfect for that. Draw right on your Snap with an adjustable line tool. Want it a different color? Use the color slider on the upper right side. Or tap the three colored circles to get one of four different color palettes—Standard full colors, Semi-transparent colors, Grayscale, and Pastels. There's also an option to draw with a line of emojis. What if you want a different size brush? No problem. Hold two fingers on the screen and move them vertically together or apart to change the size of your line. What about if you make a stray mark or a line you want to delete? There's no "drag to trash" functionality for the doodle tool, but there is an "undo" button at the top, right next to the color picker. Just tap that button and it will erase your most recent line—going all the way back to the first one if you want, one at a time. Since you are using your finger to draw on a phone screen, it's difficult to be entirely accurate with your line work, so you'll likely be using the undo feature quite a bit. But

I've also seen some Snap users create beautiful artwork with nothing more than the doodle tool.

Here's some amazing artwork from @Cyreneq and @Salliasnap

Stickers

Stickers are just what they sound like—little artistic badges to add some color and flair to your Snap. From the weird to the wonderful, there's something for every mood or moment. When you touch the sticker button, it will bring up a plethora of choices. You can browse or use the search bar to find the right option.

Recent

A list of your most recently used stickers, which is great if you have a couple of go-to stickers that you use all the time and don't want to have to track them down.

Starred

Snapchat defaults here when you open stickers. You'll find an ever-changing set of contextual stickers, related to time of day, date, current events, and other topical items. There's also a second submenu with "Smart Stickers": these add embedded functionality into the sticker. Check out the Smart Sticker section for a deeper dive into what each thing does.

Bitmoji

Here's another place where having your Bitmoji set up is essential. These stickers use your Bitmoji character right in the artwork. And when you update the outfit or hairstyle of your character (for example), they'll be updated in the Bitmoji sticker as well.

Cameos

Outside of the Giphy library of stickers, Cameos have to be some of the weirdest creations on Snapchat. Like Bitmoji, you'll have to set up your Cameo character first, but they're not a cartoon version of you: they actually use your real face in a wild, animated version of you.

Scissors

Want to create your own sticker from a picture you've taken? The scissors tool does just that. When you select the scissors tool, you can color in the area that you want to turn into a sticker, and Snapchat automatically cuts out the area it thinks you want. Because this tool is automated, for best results try to make sure you're using a plain background that's different in contrast to the subject of your sticker. That will give the app an easier time cutting out your sticker. It can be a bit of a trial-and-error process. But the results of making your own custom sticker can be incredible.

Emoji

No social media platform would be complete without giving you the opportunity to use regular Emojis. The gang's all here.

> **Quick Tip:** *Emoji Double Meaning*
>
> You're probably savvy to this already, but a quick reminder to be careful as you use emojis, because many of them have taken on double meanings in recent years—especially all the fruits and vegetables. When in doubt, a quick Internet search will tell you what a possible meaning could be.

Favorites: *"Smart Sticker"*

Under the Favorites tab, you'll get an additional submenu for adding Smart Stickers to your Snaps. These allow for additional interactivity in the Snaps you post.

GIF

Use an animated GIF from either the Snapchat, Giphy, Bitmoji, or Cameos Library.

Mention

Identical to the "@" functionality with text boxes, Mention lets you tag another user in your Snap.

Topic

Similar to Twitter's trending hashtags, Topics are chosen by Snap and pertain to timely or trending topics. Snaps posted with this sticker will be visible to anyone searching for that topic.

Location

Add your location to your Snap. Public Snaps tagged with a location also appear on the Snap Map in that spot. You can also search and tag the location of your choice.

Story

Attach a sticker that tags to one of your created stories. This can be especially useful if you're creating a Snap story that's topical and want to keep those Snaps organized. For example, you may have a particular story dedicated to your garden. When you take a Snap of those blooming zinnias, you can add your "garden story" sticker and your Snap will automatically be included when you post it.

Group

Tag a group chat that you're a part of, or you can use the sticker to create a new group by giving it a name.

General Info: *Group-Chat Stickers*

If you post a group sticker to a public story, anyone who sees that post and swipes up can join that chat.

General Info: *Screen-Element Hierarchy*

There is a hierarchy for how post-Snap elements are displayed on screen: text on the top level, then doodles, and finally stickers. Keep that in mind as you create. You'll be unable to put a sticker on top of a doodle or text. You can bring one sticker in front of the rest by selecting it and moving it slightly.

Scissors

As discussed previously, the Scissors tool allows you to cut out part of your image and use it as a sticker. All previous cutouts are saved in your sticker library.

Sounds

The Sounds tool is available to both Pre- and Post-Snaps. The only difference is that if you add your sound post-Snap, you won't be able to record your video in sync to it.

Pro Tip: *Music without Noise*

If you want cleaner audio without your background noise, be sure and use the Mute Audio button to turn off your recorded sound.

Link

This button gives you the option to add a URL to your Snap—simply type or paste your link into the search box and give Snapchat a moment to find the page. It will then generate a link sticker that includes the page headline and a preview image if that's available. Why would you want to attach a link to a Snap? There's multiple ways that this can come in handy. For example, let's say you're recording a video talking about the trailer to the latest Marvel movie; you could attach a link to the YouTube video directly in your Snap so your friends could immediately see it. Or you just bought a cute new pair of shoes and wanted to share where someone else could buy them—just attach a link in your post.

Crop

The crop tool allows you to cut down or zoom in on an area of your image. Maybe you just want to focus on one person or there's some weirdo who accidentally stepped in on the side of your image. Just simply crop out any unwanted part of the image.

PLAYBACK: *Photo*

The Playback button changes contextually depending on whether you took a photo or a video. For a photo, you can set the length of how long you want the view time of the photo. You can set the timer for intervals up to ten seconds, or Snapchat defaults to infinite—meaning the Snap will stay up until you swipe or tap on it. And as Snapchat points out, when you select this tool, only Snaps set to infinite playback time can be saved in a chat.

PLAYBACK: *Video*

When you shoot a video, the playback button changes to one of three possibilities.

Play Once

Plays your video a single time before moving to the next one.

Loop

Plays your video endlessly.

Bounce

Plays a short section of your video forward, then backward. Use the slider to adjust which part of the video gets played.

Mute Audio

Video Snaps record audio by default, but there are definitely times where you just want the video with no sound. Just hit the mute button to toggle the sound off.

General Info: *Saving With or Without Sound*

If you save a video that has sound, then hit the mute button and hit save again, it will save a new copy without audio. It will not save over the original video with sound.

Save Snap

Sometimes you create a Snap that's so awesome that you want to hang on to it. Just tap this button and (depending on your settings) a copy of the Snap will be saved to your memories and/or your camera roll. See the Profile and Settings section for further options on how to customize what happens to a saved Snap.

Memories vs. Camera Roll: What's the Difference?

On the surface, a Snap saved to your memories or your camera roll may look identical, but there is a key difference: Memories are stored on Snap's servers, and Camera Roll is saved on your phone's internal memory. So if you have a limited data plan with your phone or your phone's storage is full, you may want to go into Settings->Memories and change where your saved Snaps go.

Add to Story

This allows you to quickly add a Snap to your My Story, the Snap Map, or any other custom stories you've created—or all of the above.

Creative Tools Summary

Snapchat offers a lot of creative tools to help you express yourself. How you choose to do that is entirely up to you—your style, mood, and even what kind of day you're having can change the way you Snap. The creative tools offered are there to help you express yourself and share the moment. There are no rules that say you have to use them, but they are there if you do feel like adding a little pizzazz. I encourage you to try them out. Discover what you like and find new ways to share your story on Snapchat.

Third-Party Creative tools

Snapchat is a unique platform in that it offers access to its best features with a suite of products called Snap Kit. This allows third-party developers to integrate their app with Snapchat and create some amazing results—including ones that bring creativity back into your Snapchat story and allow you to interact with fun questions and games like "This or That" or "Never

Have I." There's quite a few to choose from, but one that I personally love to use is called Sendit. Sendit is not created by Snap, but it does integrate with your Snap story, letting you create a prompt, ask a question, or initiate a game that people can respond to. If you're trying to build an audience on Snapchat, it's a must for creating engagement.

(Full disclosure: I've known the team at Sendit for a while and I've even worked on some of the games that they have featured. That doesn't make them any less awesome.)

MESSAGING

Now that we've covered the "snap" (photo, video, and creative tools), it's time to talk about the "chat" part of Snapchat. A majority of the young people that I see using Snapchat use the chat feature as their primary messaging platform over phone calls, text messaging, or any other app. Snapchat is their go-to for firing off a quick chat with friends. Its ease of use and the fact that messages go away after viewing (unless you save them) makes Snapchat a natural choice for tech-savvy millennials and Gen Zers. Snap estimates that their users open the app on average about thirty times a day; most likely, many of those opens are in order to send and receive messages.

Perhaps you've already gotten used to using another form of communication with friends and family. Will Snapchat replace it to become your primary messaging app? That all depends. If many of the people you communicate with use Snapchat already, that's certainly a big factor. It also matters if you (and they) like using Snapchat to communicate and share. Even if it doesn't become your main method of communication, there's still a lot of fun to be had sending Snaps to your friends. You'll definitely want to know how it works and how you can get the most out of it. Let's start with the interface.

CHAT MENU

This is the main Chat menu. It is accessed from any screen by tapping on the speech bubble icon in the bottom row menu. From the Chat menu you can see whom you've communicated with and when those interactions occurred. Whether it's a text chat, or a picture or video sent to one of your friends, all of those interactions are tracked here.

Quick Tip: Notifications

If you receive a notification that someone has sent you a Snap, tapping on the notification will take you directly to the message.

A. Display name/Username
B. Message Type
C. Message Status
D. Activity Time
E. New Chat
F. Friendship Status

Display Name

This is the person you're communicating with. The Display name is what they've entered for their first and last name under their profile. This isn't necessarily their username. Along with their Display name will be the user's Bitmoji profile image, but only if they have their Bitmoji set up. From this menu, if you tap on someone's username, it will open the direct chat window with that person. We'll cover the direct chat window more in the next section.

Hidden Feature:

Tapping on another user's Profile image will take you to your friendship profile with that person. This screen gives you more information about your contact, including saved chats, attachments, and charms. Check out the Friendship Profiles section for more information.

Message Type

Snapchat recognizes several different types of messages sent to other users. They're even color-coded shapes so you know what type of message you last exchanged:

Blue chat shape: Basic Text Chat, Sticker, Cameo, or saved video sent through chat
Red square: Still image or Video Snap without Sound
Purple square: Video Snap with Sound
If it's a message you sent, it will just be a solid arrow in the color of the mes-

sage type—blue, red, or purple. And once the message is opened by the recipient, it will revert back to the chat or square shape outline.

Gray arrow: This is used when you send a message to someone who hasn't accepted your friend request, depending on their privacy settings.

Replay Icon: If someone replays your video Snap, you'll see a circular arrow icon, indicating that they watched it again.

Message Status

If you're not into trying to figure out what the color shapes mean, the message status gives an easily understandable text description of the status of your message.

▶ Delivered: Your message was sent,but not opened.

▷ Opened: Your message was sent, and opened by the recipient.

■ or ◾ New Snap: Someone sent you a Snap message or video, but you haven't opened it yet.

□ or ◻ Received and opened: You opened the message from a sender. After watching a Snap, you'll have a few seconds to touch and hold to reload the Snap to play again. If you exit the chat or wait too long, the Snap is gone for good.

▷ Screenshot: You took a screenshot of a Snap, the chat window, or even your friend's profile.

○ Replay: Someone replayed your message.

Hidden Feature: *Screenshots and Screen Recordings*

Snapchat was originally conceived as the "disappearing messages" app, so privacy was built into the premise. But this meant if one user could secretly screenshot or screen-record while using the app, that would defeat the concept of privacy. Fortunately, Snapchat can identify if someone has taken a screenshot or screen recording of the chat, your Snap, or even your profile and will give you a message that it has happened.

Activity Time

This is just a quick note of when you last sent or received a Snap from the user.

New Chat

Tap this button to start a new conversation. When you hit this button, it opens up your Contacts and lets you select a single person, multiple individuals, or groups. You can even create a new group chat. There's lots to unpack with Group Chats, so before you start one, make sure you read the section on them.

Friend Emojis

These are emoji icons that appear next to profiles that you regularly or constantly communicate with.

Super BFF: You've been best friends with this person for 2 consecutive months.

BFF: You've been best friends for 2 consecutive weeks.

Besties: You are each other's best friend. You both send the most Snaps to each other.

BFs: You send a lot of Snaps to this person, but they're not your #1.

Mutual Besties: Your #1 best friend is also their #1 best friend. (See the Profile section for more about your Best Friends.)

Mutual BFs: One of your best friends is also this person's best friend.

Streaks

You can hardly spend any amount of time on Snapchat without hearing about Snap streaks or just Streaks. If you send a Snap to the same person every day for at least 3 consecutive days, Snapchat will give you a 🔥 emoji with a number indicating how many days in a row you've been Snapping with this person. Both Snapchatters have a 24-hour window each day to send a new Snap to each other to keep it alive. If the streak is about to expire, you'll see a ⌛ emoji next to their name in the chat menu.

Remember that only new Snaps count toward your streaks. This doesn't count Snaps sent from Memories or Spectacles content; so if you're wanting to continue your streaks, exchange an original Snap!

Hot Tip: *To Streak or Not*

Some people (like yours truly) aren't really big on Streaks. No judgment if you do love them, but it's just not for me. Make sure if you do want to start Streaks with a friend that they are on board with the idea. Don't just spam them with streaks, because that gets old fast. And never send streaks to anyone you're not friends with. I can guarantee they will not appreciate it.

Direct Chat Window

A. Display name and Bitmoji profile image
B. Voice and Video call
C. Back button
D. Chat window
E. Take a Snap
F. Text box
G. Voice record
H. Stickers
I. Memories and Camera Roll
J. Snap Games and Minis

After tapping on someone's name or starting a new chat and selecting a contact, you'll be taken to the Direct Chat window. This is where all the actual back-and-forth messaging functions happen. On this screen, you can send text, pictures, audio, video, and stickers; make calls; and even play games. There's a lot going on with this screen, so let's dive in and see what each thing does.

Display Name and Bitmoji Profile Image

This is the person you're talking to. Just like anywhere else in Snapchat, if you tap on their profile image, you'll be taken to your friendship profile page. See the Friendship Profile section to learn lots more about this.

Voice and Video Call

This functionality works just like a phone call or video chat right inside the Snapchat app. This also works with group chats for up to fifteen people. Calls on Snapchat don't count against your phone minutes for your wireless plan (but they will use your data if you're not connected to Wi-Fi).

Here's a quick rundown of what the various buttons do when a call is active.

A. Incoming feed. If you're on a voice call, this
B. circle is an audio visualizer. And in a video call, it becomes the video feed. Tapping on the video will make this input go full-screen. In full-screen mode, swipe down to go back to the chat window.

C. Outgoing feed. This is what you're putting out there, either an audio visualizer for voice call, or your camera feed for video calls. You can tap on this circle to bring your own video up larger as well. It will display as a bigger circle in the lower part of the screen.

D. Speakerphone mode.

E. Mute microphone.

F. Turn on the camera and instantly turn your voice call into a video call. But note that this button turns on only your own camera and you'll both need to activate it to be full video.

G. Chat toolbar: Even though you're already conversing live, you can still keep the chat window going with funny stickers, memories, or even just text.

H. End call. When you're done yappin'. "No, YOU hang up first!"

I. Colorful "Live call" indicator. Just a friendly reminder that you're still connected to someone. Helpful during those long, awkward silences. Or when you're doing long-distance meditation exercises.

If your device is locked, a Snapchat call will ring your phone just like a regular phone call. Your screen will show the caller's name and say what type of Snapchat call it is (audio or video). You can answer the call right from the lock screen or hit the Snapchat button to open it in the app. And on iOS devices, your phone will track these in your regular phone-call log.

Hidden Feature: *Automatic Speakerphone*

In a voice call, Snapchat will automatically change to speakerphone mode if you take your phone away from your face. Put the phone back to your ear to hear it through the normal earpiece. Of course, if you're using a Bluetooth headset for audio, that will take precedence over all else.

Back Button

This is how to get out of the Direct Chat screen and back to the Chat menu. Just be careful as you tap, since this button is very close to the video call button and it's easy to "fat-finger" and accidentally start a call with someone that you didn't intend to. Nothing strikes fear in the hearts of people more than seeing that "Calling Bernice..." message pop up when you didn't intend to call her. Then you gotta explain that it was a mistake and it becomes a whole thing.

Hidden Feature: *Slide Back*

If you're not really a "Back Button" kinda person, you can also swipe left on this screen to get back to the Chat menu.

Chat Window

Here is where your Chats, Snaps, Stickers, and more are displayed—same as many other chat windows that you're probably familiar with. But there is a key difference in Snapchat: by default, your messages delete after you view them (and close out of the Direct Chat window). So if you read something and go back to the Chat menu, they'll have been instantly vaporized.

Hot Tip: *Delete After 24 Hours*

I actually like my messages in Snapchat to stick around for a bit longer. It gives me more time to come up with my witty repartee. Fortunately, there's a feature that allows you to keep them for 24 hours. Tap your friend's Bitmoji/Story icon to go to their Friendship profile, and then tap the three dots in the upper right corner. In that menu, find "Delete Chats" halfway down. Change this setting to "24 Hours After Viewing" to make your texts stick around for a little while longer at least.

Hidden Feature: *Timestamps*

The chat window is organized in ascending order for how your Snaps are organized. If you have saved Snaps in the chat, you'll also see a date line below it—or it will say "Yesterday" or "Today" if they're much more recent. But there's another feature that lets you see the exact time you send or receive a Snap. All you have to do is hold down on the chat window and pull to the right. You'll see the timestamps for each Snap appear beside them in this hidden tray.

Replaying Snaps

Did someone send you a Snap that went by too quickly or that you want to see again? There's a very short period in which you're able to do this. After watching the Snap, but still in the open Chat window, you'll see a "Hold to Replay" message below the Snap. Touch and hold down to rewind and play it again. But be quick! You only have a few short seconds to activate it. And once the replay option goes away, that Snap is gone for good.

Take a Snap

Tap this to activate the camera. Get creative and send your most creative Snap.

Hidden Feature: *Friend's Birthday Lenses*

On your friend's birthday, there are special Lenses you'll be able to access when you take a Snap from within their Direct Chat box.

Text Box

When you're typing out a message, your text appears here. Hey, you know how a text window works!

Activity Indicator

Have you noticed a little Bitmoji guy pop up when you're typing a message? That means the other person you're talking to is in the Chat window with you. If their Bitmoji is just peeking over the edge, they are just waiting. But if you see the Bitmoji pop up with a little speech bubble, that means the other person is typing in the chat window. The same is true on their end as well.

General Info: *Chat Activity Indicator*

The activity Bitmoji indicator only works for people who have their Bitmoji set up.

Voice Recording

This handy feature allows you to record an audio message and send it directly. This is great if you're trying to explain something and typing everything out takes too long. Just hold down on the microphone button in the Chat window and talk away. Remember that this is different from the text-to-speech function that modern phones have with the keyboard.

Hidden Feature: *Deleting a Voice Recording In Progress*

If you're in the middle of a recording and you want to delete what you've got, just keep your finger on the button and swipe left.

Stickers

Most of the same Stickers that you can use in creating your Snaps are also available in the Chat window as well. This includes recently used Stickers, Bitmoji, Cameos, Snap-created Stickers, and even your custom ones that you cut out with the Scissors tool. The only ones you can't see here are Stickers from the Giphy library.

Hidden Feature: *Contextual Stickers*

If you start typing, Snapchat will automatically suggest a contextual Sticker to use based on what you're writing. It pops up in the place of the Smiley Face icon.

Memories and Camera Roll

You can also send saved Snaps and videos from your camera roll directly into the Chat. They appear differently in the Chat than typical Snaps. Whereas a regular Snap will either show up as a red or purple square in the Chat window that you can tap on to see full-screen, saved Snaps, videos, and pictures show up and play automatically as a smaller version within the Chat itself. You can still tap on the video to bring it up full-screen (with sound if that's available). An additional feature that you don't get with regular Snaps is having the ability to save another person's video from the Chat to your own Memories or camera roll.

Hidden Feature: *Saving Items in the Chat*

Even if you have your Snaps set to disappear immediately, you can still save certain items indefinitely. Just tap on the text, saved video/memory, recorded audio, or sticker you want to save and it will briefly slide to the right with a little message that says "Saved." It will get a light gray background to let you know it's saved. And if you don't want something saved any longer, just tap it again and it will get a message saying "unsaved."

For any item in the Chat, there is a submenu that you can access by pressing and holding down on the item of interest. It is contextual depending on whether it is text, audio, or video. This gives you a few more options for that adorable picture of a cat cleaning its paw that you saved in the Chat window, because it is so cute and it must be shared.

This shows what a saved image or video looks like in the Chat. It tells you who sent it and what time. It also lets you unsave the image, even if you weren't the person who saved it. And you can also export a picture or video and save it to your phone's camera roll. Hitting Snap Reply turns that picture into a Sticker placed in a Snap reply directly to your friend. So you can tell them specifically how adorable that cat licking its paw is, with the picture right there, so they know which of the many, many cat pictures you've sent is the one you're talking about.

Saved items will appear here in the Direct Chat window the next time you open it, even if you have Snaps set to delete after viewing. Also these saved videos, pictures, and Chat attachments will show up in a section on your Friendship Profile.

Snap Games and Minis

Tapping the little rocket-ship icon here opens up the Snap Games and Minis menu. These are a bunch of multiplayer games and activities you can do with your friends, created by partner game studios and organizations.

Games

Unlike the games that appear in the Lens Carousel, Snap games are real-time multiplayer games. There's a long list of games with new ones being added all the time, so I won't get into each game in this book, but I definitely recommend you check them out.

Hot Tip: *Game Group Chat*

Start a Group chat specifically for your friends that are down to play Snap Games. It's a quick way to get into the action—and, as the old multiplayer gamer saying goes, "the more, the merrier!"

Minis

While Snap Games are just for fun, Snap Minis actually help you. Many of these Minis are created in partnership with experts in the industry to help teach you investing, cooking, or meditation. There are Snap Minis that help you buy movie tickets, make a decision about what activity you and your friends want to do, study for a test, or even register to vote.

Group Chats

Chatting with a single person is a great way to get to know somebody. But sometimes you want to be in the mix with a bunch of friends. The free-flowing conversation, random subject changes, and the chance for every-one to get in on a joke are perfect for a group chat. Any chat that has more than two people in it is considered a group chat, and they're very easy to get started.

Just click the "New Chat" button from the Chat menu and select two or more people and start the Chat—that's it. Or go into your Contacts and hit the New Group + button. You can give the group a name at the top, which you should definitely do if you've formed this chat for a reason, even if that reason is "People who love 80s movies" or "Corgi pals."

Hot Tip: *Invite by URL*

You can invite other people to your group chat from a URL link as well. After you hit the New Group + button, it will change to say "Invite to Group via Link." Give this group a name (required) and then you can send out this new link through all your phone shortcuts—email, text, Twitter, Facebook. Honestly I can't imagine the group that would form from an open link via Twitter, but if you're crazy enough to try it, more power to you!

If you made a group with a few members and would like to add more, that's easy enough. Tap on the Bitmoji profile circle in the top left. That should already have multiple Bitmojis for your friends that are in the group. That will take you to the group Profile page (very similar to a friendship Profile mentioned earlier) that has information about the people in the group, in-cluding a Snap Map location for everyone who is sharing that information.

Now you can tap the three dots in the top right corner for a Settings menu for this chat. Here you can do things like leave the group, change the group name, pin or clear conversations, and at the bottom add members to the group. Hitting that button will take you to your Contacts or to get a URL link for your group.

Something to take note of is that once you form a group chat, you can't delete it. Why not? you may ask. Well, once the group is made, it isn't yours anymore. It belongs to everyone in that group. All you can really do is leave the group if you don't want to be a part of it anymore. You also can't kick anyone out of the group either. So be careful about who you invite to your group!

My wife and daughters recently took a road trip to another state to visit extended family, leaving me home to work on this book. Even though they were on the road, I was able to use Snapchat to keep track of their progress. I did it by having my daughter share her location with me, using Snap Map. Every time she checked in on Snapchat, I was able to follow their progress and make sure they made it to their destination. Not only that, but I could see my daughter's fun road trip Snaps as she posted her story. So even though I couldn't go with them, I was still along for the ride.

The Snap Map occupies a prominent place in the main navigation, but in my opinion it is a quite useful and rather under-utilized feature. Assuming that you're allowing Snapchat to use your location data, the Snap Map will show you where you are on a world map. It will also show your friends' locations who are also sharing that info with you (not everyone may be comfortable sharing that). Let's take a quick look at key parts of the Snap Map.

A. City/Region
B. My Bitmoji
C. Recenter on Me
D. Friends
E. Friends' Location
F. Points of Interest
G. Snap Heat Map
H. Settings

City/Region

This tells you what area of the map you are looking at. It changes dynamically as you scroll around. If you're scrolling over a particular region and you notice a yellow circle with an image in this block, you can tap on it to get a sample of local public Snaps from this area. You'll also notice local temperature and a symbol for the weather condition.

My Bitmoji

A quick-access panel to update your Bitmoji's action or activity. Some people like to set their Bitmoji to show what they're actually doing. So whether
it's stopping for coffee, playing football, or just listening to music, you can
use your Bitmoji to indicate to your friends what you are up to. There's also
an option that takes you to the Bitmoji edit screen so you can change its
appearance or clothing as well.

Recenter on me

If you've been scrolling around the map and have lost where your location
is, just tap this button to recenter the map on your own Bitmoji.

Friends

This is really a key feature for the Snap Map. Not only can you find your
friends by location using the map itself, but the Friends button brings up a
list of your friends who've had some recent activity. Use the Search button
if you're looking for a particular person. Then tap on your friend's profile image to zoom in on their location. Check the list below the Find Your Friends
section to see who has been traveling. And scroll down even farther to get
Snapchat highlights from events, sports, and points of interest from around
the world. These are Snaps sourced from regular Snapchat users who've
used the location tag or filter for an event.

Friend's Location

Looking for one of your Snapchat friends to hang out with? You can easily
see who is nearby you on your Snap Map. These Bitmojis on the Snap
Map represent your friend's location the last time they opened Snapchat. If
you can't find a particular friend, or they can't find you, that's because the
privacy settings you have set up don't allow it. If there's someone you want
to share your location with in Snapchat, find their name and hit the "Share
my location" link.

Point of Interest

As you explore the map, Snapchat has highlighted certain locations you may find interesting. If you see a specialized icon (like the Hollywood sign, for example), tap on it for more information like directions, busy times, and hours of operation. You can even send this location to one of your Contacts if you and some friends are trying to meet up somewhere.

If you zoom in to particular regions of the map, Snapchat will also display stores, restaurants, museums, clubs, and parks. The Snap Map encourages real-world engagement with the people you like to hang out with by showing the fun things to do in your area. Tapping on one of these locations will give you additional information about it, like hours of operation, address, phone number, website, and popular times. You can send the address to a friend through Snapchat or to your navigation app, which will give you directions to get there.

Snap Heat Map

As you're scrolling through the map, you'll probably notice little multi-colored clouds in certain areas. This isn't a Doppler radar display of precipitation: it's actually a "heat map" for where people are posting Snaps. You'll notice they're a particularly intense red color around big cities, with a higher density of people posting to Snapchat there. You can even tap on one of these little colorful clouds to see local public Snaps posted in an area. Now you can check out what locals are posting from Paris, France, to Paris, Texas.

Settings

I'm sure the more privacy-minded among you see the Snap Map as something that makes you sweat a bit, but not to worry: you can easily and quickly change your location setting here. Tapping on the gear will bring up the Settings menu, where you can update who can (or cannot) see your location. You can go into Ghost Mode, making you invisible to everyone on the map, if you're doing some Covert Ops–type stuff and want to vanish for a bit.

There are also options to report issues, or suggest a place for Snap to add to the map. Remember that even with your security setting set to default, only the people who you're Snapchat friends with will be able to see your location.

Pro Tip: *Snap Map on Snapchat.com*

The Snap Map is one of the many features that you can access off the Snapchat app by going to Snapchat.com and clicking on the Map navigation tab. Here you browse what's going on around the entire world on Snapchat. View Snaps from major sporting events, concerts, and famous locations. Or just see what's happening in your local area.

Pro Tip for Parents

I highly recommend that you make sure any of your children who use Snapchat turn on Location Sharing with you. They may feel like it's an invasion of privacy to them, but it's a little peace of mind for you—and it's not a bad thing to be able to check on their location from time to time.

Many people know me as "The guy who made the Potato," but how did this Lens actually take over the Internet? Early in the pandemic lockdown, we were all finding quirky new ways to make the best of an awful situation. It was in between learning how to make my own pickles and coming to the realization that my home office was insufficiently soundproofed for having my children "distance learning" that an amazing thing happened. As most people were working from home and doing virtual meetings, they desired to make the meetings more fun and turned to using Snap Camera to add augmented reality effects to their webcam feeds. One such meeting achieved viral fame on Twitter, when a woman tweeted a picture of her boss who activated a Snapchat Lens that she couldn't figure out how to turn off and ended up participating in the rest of the meeting as a potato. The post about "Potato Boss" was retweeted almost a million times and made news cycles around the world. Soon the potato was a cultural phenomenon—getting referenced by late-night show hosts, the answer in an NPR quiz show, an Internet catchphrase ("un-potato me!"), and even the punch line for a joke on a prime-time sitcom. The potato then went on to star in a marketing campaign for Taco Bell when they were announcing the return of their vegetarian options (like potato burritos). It was kinda shocking that the potato in question was none other than the Snapchat Lens I created. All that to say, there's something magical about a Snapchat Lens. They have the potential to make the world smile.

Snapchat Lenses are a huge topic—and one that's near and dear to me as a Lens Creator. It's my livelihood and my passion. Before I started making Lenses a couple of years ago, Augmented Reality felt like something that only highly trained and skilled teams of professionals could do—and for a long time, that was the case. But since Snapchat launched their free software called Lens Studio, they've made it possible for creatives, programmers, and hobbyists of every skill level to be able to create their own. The really great thing is that all those Lenses that people around the world have made are available right in Snapchat.

AUGMENTED REALITY

I've mentioned the term Augmented Reality (or AR) several times already, but what does it actually mean? What is Augmented Reality, and how does it work? At the most basic level, Augmented Reality utilizes computer-generated imagery to add to the "real-world" view on your screen. It takes input from the camera, and in conjunction with additional sensors like gyroscope, accelerometer, microphone, GPS data, and secondary camera lenses, creates a heightened experience for the user.

The AR software takes all the input from the camera and other sensors, and uses Machine Learning (a type of Artificial Intelligence, or AI) to get an understanding of the scene. Many of the things our brains do automatically, like understanding depth and recognizing objects, have to be trained and programmed into the software. This allows the software to look at live video and quickly know things like where the ground plane is, what is a person's face, which part is the sky, whether the person is smiling—just to name a few. With that information, AR can then track computer-generated imagery to something in the scene and make it look like it's actually there. Those dog ears and nose on your face, a painted mural come to life with animation, or a 3D scale model of the Eiffel Tower placed on the ground in front of you are examples of the powerful AI hard at work. And that's really the magic of Augmented Reality.

FILTERS AND LENSES: *What's the Difference?*

So, are they Snapchat filters or Lenses, and what's the difference? Many people refer to all the AR experiences on Snapchat as filters. Snap makes the distinction that a filter is a simple image overlay on top of the view without any additional experiential elements to it. So a filter could contain just a sticker, GIF, or text. Filters can be geofenced to a particular area or during certain dates, and are great for special occasions like celebrating a wedding or graduation. Users can make their own custom filters at Snapchat.com/create.

A Snapchat Lens, on the other hand, is much more in-depth. Lenses can use the full AR capabilities to create interactive experiences—everything from changing the user's hair color, adding flying whales to the sky, or my personal favorite: turning the user into a potato. Lenses are interactive and dynamic, and they utilize some type of scene understanding to work.

Once you know the distinction, it's pretty easy to tell the difference between a filter and a Lens. And while it is technically correct to call the AR experiences on Snapchat "Lenses," other platforms call them filters and most people know them as that.

LENS DISCOVERY

So now that you know the difference, let's talk about all the awesome Lens experiences waiting for you on Snapchat. To activate Lens mode from the camera screen, simply tap on the face button to the right of the main Record Snap button. This will bring up the Lens Carousel menu.

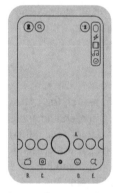

A. Lens Carousel
B. Create
C. Scan
D. Browse
E. Explore
F. Camera View

Lens Carousel (Browse)

This is the primary selection of Lenses that Snapchat curates. They're where the average Snapchatter will start when they're looking for Lenses. Some are advertisements, like the first Lens that comes up. Most if not all of these carousel Lenses will be created by the Snapchat team, so they'll be top quality. It's possible to find some community-created Lenses mixed in here as well.

General info: *Browse Button*

By default, Snapchat opens the Lens Carousel on the Browse page. If you're using Scan or Create and want to go back to the regular Lens Carousel, just hit the browse button.

Hidden Feature: *Activating Lenses*

Even though there is a button dedicated to activating Lenses, a secondary and faster way is to just tap anywhere on the screen. This will bring up the Lens Carousel and associated action menu.

Create

These are Snapchat-made Lenses that have an additional creative feature to them that puts you in charge of the resulting experience. This can be any-thing from screen scanner, makeup builder, or background video, to face morph. The point of these Lenses is to allow you to make your own custom Lens experience inside the Lens itself. Many of these also have a yellow camera button that gives you a countdown before it starts recording, allow-ing you to do a hands-free or full-body video.

Scan

One of the coolest things about Snapchat is this built-in search tool. At its most basic level, the Scan tool will look at whatever is on-screen and serve you up a Snapchat Lens based on whatever's there. If it's your face, then a nice selfie Lens could show up. If it's your dog, Snapchat will give you a Lens that works on pets. Snapchat's machine learning algorithms are already programmed to detect thousands of objects, so it's really fun to see what Snapchat comes up with for a recommendation.

Hidden Feature: *Quick Activate Scan*

You can easily activate the Scan from the main screen by doing a long press on the screen. The Scan button also appears when you activate the Lens Carousel screen; the Scan button will show up in the Chat button's place.

Where Scan really shines is in its specialized scanning tools. Product scan will return Amazon listings for whatever you scan. Music scan uses Shazam to determine the song that's playing. Math Solver connects to Photomath to give you answers to the math problem you're staring at. Dog scanner can give you a dog's breed with a percentage of accuracy. Plant Snap does the same, except with vegetation. Vehicle scanner tells you the make and model of the vehicle you're looking at, along with price and a link to learn more. With Nutrition scan, you can scan a product's barcode and it uses Yuka.io which goes beyond just giving you calories, fats, and sugar info: it actually tells you positives and negatives about the product and an overall rating. It's really helpful if you're being careful about what you eat. And finally, Wine scan integrates with Vivino, so when you scan a wine label it gives you more information about that bottle, a five-star rating, and average price.

I'm sure as time goes on, Snapchat will add lots more scanning possibilities, but even what's there now is really impressive.

Explore

My very favorite part of Snapchat. This page is where you can browse the many Lenses made by Snapchat, the creator community, and AR enthusiasts around the world. There are categories for the different types of Lenses, like Face, World, Music, Trending, and For You. Don't miss the Creators tab at the end of the list to see great Lenses from your favorite creators.

And under the For You section is a list of all the Lenses that you've favorited, so you can quickly access them again. To use a Lens from the list, just tap on its preview or icon to activate. If you do a long press on a Lens preview, it brings up another menu with more information and options. Here you can see the name of the Lens and its creator. You can favorite the Lens by tapping on the heart icon. Report a Lens if it's inappropriate. Subscribe to the creator of the Lens, or view their profile, which will have a complete list of their other Lenses. You can also copy the link to the Lens so you can save it as a link or use it in any way you might with a URL. Or send the Lens directly to one of your Snapchat friends.

Hot Tip: *Voice Scan*

Inside Lens Explorer (if you have Voice Scan activated in your Settings), you can tap on the microphone icon in the search bar and just say what kind of Lens you want or the effect you're looking for. You can say things like "Turn me into a cockroach" or "Make my hair pink," and Snapchat will come up with a selection of Lenses that do just that. Note that voice scan doesn't work in all regions.

Hot Tip: *Subscriptions*

If you find a Lens Creator whose work you like, don't forget to sub-scribe to them. Then when they release new Lenses, you'll be the first to know. It will also help you get to know the person behind the work: many of the Lens Creators in the community are awesome, interesting, and funny people who appreciate your patronage. We make Lenses because we love it and love how people react to our work. Your subscription lets us know we're doing a good job.

Hot Tip: *View Lens Page*

A real hidden gem inside Snapchat is the Lens page. Here you can see a collection of all the spotlight Snaps that have been created using a particular Lens. Not every Lens has a page, but for those that do, it's fun to go in and see what Snaps people have created using that Lens—some are quite hilarious.

Using Lenses

You've probably learned by now that there isn't just one type of Snapchat Lens. In fact, there are dozens of different major categories with nearly endless possibilities for customization. All that is to say, when you open a Lens in Snapchat, your experience could be almost anything. Snapchat has created Machine Learning-driven experiences that can make you look like a living Disney character or a Norman Rockwell painting. Others have built interactive games that you can play using the world around you. There are now even connected Lenses that create a persistent shared experience by multiple Snapchat users on their own devices. Here are a few suggestions for getting the most out of your Lens experience.

Face or World

Since every AR experience has to happen on your phone screen (or Spec-tacles), and your smartphone has either a front- or back-facing camera, we can divide all Lenses into either Face (Front-facing camera) or World (Back-facing camera). And even with that, there are some caveats—some have experiences that use both cameras, and there is an entire subset of Lenses that work specifically for Spectacles.

But as far as Face and World Lenses go—if you have the front-facing camera active, Snapchat will automatically filter out world experiences from the Carousel. Best practices for Lens designers are for them to give you on-screen instructions to flip your camera to view the experience, and to select which camera their Lens is ideally suited for when they create the Lens. But if you're trying a Lens that seems to be doing nothing or is behaving oddly, try flipping the camera to see if the intended experience is on the other camera view.

Good Lenses should also give you instructions on how to activate any of the action triggers for the AR experience. This could be anything from raising your eyebrows, to smiling, to opening your mouth. Not all Lenses have an experience trigger, but if it does, hopefully the designer included a clue for you to activate it.

Hot Tip: *Favorites and Lens Information*

With a Lens active, at the bottom of the screen will be a Heart button, which you can use to quickly add this Lens to your favorites.

Additionally, you will find an Info button in the upper left, which will display the Lens name and creator. Tapping on that will bring up the Lens information menu, identical to the one in Explorer when you long-press on a Lens icon.

Full Body

Snapchat has the ability to track your entire body in 3D, and Lens Creators have made some incredible experiences using this technology. The key to making this work, however, is that enough of your body has to be in view of the camera in order for it to track you. This is much easier in the back camera, because you can just point it at another person, but if you want it to work on yourself, it will involve propping up your camera somewhere and possibly using the Timer tool to record yourself.

Image Marker

Image marker Lenses are looking for a specific image to trigger an AR experience. All these Lenses should give you an on-screen example of the image that they're looking for, and hopefully the target image is near at hand or common enough that you'll be able to point your camera at it and activate the experience.

For a fun example of this, I created a unique image marker experience that triggers from a ten-dollar bill. It was not long after Lin Manuel Miranda's *Hamilton* Broadway show had made its way into our house that my teenage daughter had its songs playing on repeat. I had the idea that it might be fun to make Alexander himself sing a snippet of the namesake track. Technically, it was a unique challenge to figure out how to do it, and the resulting experience turned out better than I could have hoped. So great, in fact, that Snap used a video of it in the keynote speech for their first Snap Partner Summit. And it's been continually used as an exemplar of Image Marker technology ever since. Try it with an actual ten-dollar bill (or the image of one).

Lens link here:

Landmarker

These are Lenses that only work at particular locations around the world. They trigger on the geometry of a particular building or structure and create an experience around it. If you live near or visit these locations, it's definitely worth opening Snapchat and seeing what interesting AR creations have been made for these places.

Current list of locations:

1 - US Capitol Building, Washington, DC, USA
2 - TCL Chinese Theater, Hollywood, CA, USA
3 - Flatiron Building, New York City, NY, USA
4 - Buckingham Palace, London, UK
5 - Eiffel Tower, Paris, France
6 - Arc de Triomphe, Paris, France
7 - El Castillo, Yucatan, Mexico
8 - Galata Tower, Istanbul, Turkey
9 - Gateway to India, Mumbai, India
10 - Great Sphinx of Giza, Giza, Egypt
11 - Leaning tower of Piza, Piza, Italy
12 - Natural History Museum, London, UK
13 - Neues Rathaus, Munich, Germany
14 - Prague Astronomical Clock, Prague, Czech Republic
15 - Qasr Al Farid, Mada'in Salih, Saudi Arabia
16 - Statue of Liberty, New York City, NY, USA
17 - Taj Mahal, Agra, India
18 - Tower Bridge, London, UK
19 - National Gallery, London, UK
20 - Palacio De Bellas Artes, Mexico City, Mexico
21 - Royal Palace, Oslo, Norway
22 - Stortinget, Oslo, Norway
23 - Colosseum, Rome, Italy
24 - Altare della Patria, Rome, Italy
25 - Juliet's Balcony, Verona, Italy
26 - Town Hall, Brussels, Belgium
27 - Royal Palace, Amsterdam, Netherlands
28 - Rijksmuseum (Canal side & Park side), Amsterdam, Netherlands
29 - Reichstag, Berlin, Germany
30 - Brandenburg Gate, Berlin, Germany

Lenses Summary

Snap and its community of Lens Creators are constantly pushing the boundaries of what is possible with Augmented Reality. Using these Lenses can not only help you create more interesting Snaps, but they can also better connect you to the people in your lives. I'm obviously biased, but I say that the place for consistently finding the best and most innovative Augmented Reality is on Snapchat.

SNAP CAMERA

I'd be remiss if I wrote an entire book about Snapchat without talking a bit about Snap Camera. It's a separate program you can download from snapcamera.snapchat.com that installs on your computer and lets you activate Snapchat Lenses right on your webcam video stream. Remember the whole Potato Boss thing? That was using Snap Camera. There are a ton of Twitch and YouTube streamers who use it for adding AR effects to their broadcasts. Streamers like it because Snap Camera gives you a horizontal screen-based activation for Snapchat Lenses, instead of portrait mode. You can use Snap Camera in conjunction with streaming broadcast software like OBS to create more polished, professional-looking streams with the added flair of interactive visual effects. Many of the Lenses that I've created have become streamers' favorites and account for a big part of the popularity of my Lenses.

Snap Camera has also enabled new forms of entertainment. At the start of the pandemic, many in the entertainment industry were left scrambling to figure out how to carry on production with people unable to be near each other and other restrictions. Snap Camera actually provided a unique solution for one show. Nickelodeon's *Unfiltered* is a first-of-its-kind game show taking place entirely over webcams to create a zany, hilarious program that utilizes Snapchat augmented reality Lenses to maximum effect. On the show, the three kid contestants try to guess who the mystery celebrity is who is disguised behind a Snapchat Lens. Snap Camera became the perfect solution to solving a production challenge and became a great example of how Augmented Reality is creating new art forms. If you haven't seen Nickelodeon's *Unfiltered* yet, I recommend it, not only to see what's possible, but also because I work on the show and have created many of its featured Snapchat Lenses.

After you've used Snapchat for a bit and had fun with all the augmented reality effects, you're probably wondering if you might be able to create your own filters and Lenses. The answer is absolutely!

On Snapchat.com, there are pages dedicated to both filters and Lenses. Anyone can create amazing high-end AR Lenses with Lens Studio—and there's lots of great documentation to guide you through the process. But it does require a computer and, oftentimes, some additional software. On the other hand, creating your own filters can be done right from Snapchat's website with their online filter-building tools (which will cost you a few bucks to publish). These are perfect for making a unique custom filter for your special social event, such as a wedding, graduation, or birthday party. There's a free filter option available too, called Community Filters, which will allow you to upload your own design.

Pro Tip: *Creator Marketplace and Lens Web Builder*

If you're a business looking to get a Snapchat Lens made, I first recommend that you come to me or one of the many talented creators in the Snap Lens Network. Go to ar.snap.com/creatormarketplace to find many talented individuals and studios (and yours truly) ready to create a premium Snapchat Lens experience for you.

And if you're looking for something quick and a little more "off the shelf," check out Snapchat's Lens Web Builder, which is an online creation tool with multiple Lens templates ready to go. Just add a logo and you're set!

COMMUNITY FILTERS

Like the name suggests, Community filters are intended to be enjoyed by everyone. They can either be a Geofilter, which will have you cordon them off to a specific area on a map, or a Moment filter, which will deliver your filter more contextually, based on your choice from a menu of options. For example, certain filters appear only when the user is taking a selfie, at a concert, or bedtime. Both will require you to have some type of graphic-design or photo-editing software to create it, so you can save out your design with a transparent background and size it to the proper dimensions of 1080px x 2340px. There's also an approval process where your design is vetted by Snapchat. Your filter design will need to be original artwork, content-specific to your type of submission (meaning localized to the geographic area, or appropriate to the event/moment) and meeting certain technical requirements. It also has to be deemed interesting or useful, which is sorta vague and open to interpretation. So if you make a design that has a space monkey saying "Congratulations" and localize it to your hometown, odds are your filter submission will be rejected.

ONLINE FILTER CREATOR

Let's briefly explore the creation process using Snap's online filter-building tools. Start by going to Snapchat.com/create and selecting Filters (not Community Filters). You'll log in with your Snapchat account. You'll see a screen that looks like this:

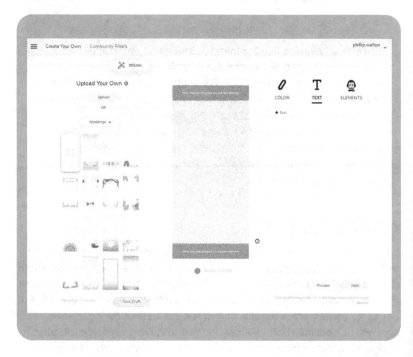

If you've already created your design (following their technical requirements), you can just upload it directly. Or choose your type of event, which will give you different background overlay designs. Select a background or leave it blank. Then use the color and the text to create the message for your filter. You can also add Bitmoji stickers of yourself or any of your friends. Make sure you position all your screen elements like text and stickers within the light gray area so it will display nicely on every screen size. When you're happy with the design, hit NEXT and choose the dates and times when you want it to be available. After that, you'll choose the geographic location where it will be available. Start by searching for a location; then you'll have to draw out a Geofence for where it will go. Only Snapchatters within that Geofence will be served your filter. A Geofence must be under 50 million square feet, which sounds like a lot, but is smaller than you'd think. Click "Draw Fence" and click on the map to create your Geofence. If the area you drew is green, you're good to go. You'll see the square footage and the cost of your Geofence in the upper right corner of your screen. Then all you have to do is go to checkout and pay with a credit card. Cost varies by location and the size of your Geofence, so be as specific as possible.

SEARCH

It's safe to assume that you already know how to use a search bar, but there are a couple of features within Snapchat that are worth pointing out. Snapchat's search feature is not just for finding other Snapchat users. It also provides additional recommendations from across Snapchat. Tap on the search bar magnifying glass or swipe down to activate it.

Best Friends

In this section you'll find your Snapchat friends who you've been talking to and sharing Snaps with the most. You'll also see your friendship emoji status with this person as well.

Recents

This is a list of your recent searches that you've tapped on. So if you added a friend, used a Lens, subscribed to a verified account, or just sent a Snap to a friend, it will be listed here in the order that it happened.

Happening Now

Snapchat will automatically populate this list with news and current events from around the world and the Internet that you might be interested in.

Games and Minis

This is a recommended list of games, activities, shopping, and fun within Snapchat.

Quick Add

These are people that Snapchat thinks you may know or want to add as friends. They could be people who share a number of mutual friends (which Snapchat will let you know) or people who are found in your Contacts.

TRENDING

This is a list of popular people, Lenses, and shows on Snapchat. Check it out for the latest things people are buzzing about.

Hidden Feature: *Search Topics*

When you start typing a word into the Search box, Snapchat will immediately begin to recommend results. On that list, in addition to the friends, shows, verified accounts, and Lenses, will be locations from the Snap Map and Topics.

Topics are taken from the hashtags of the video Snaps submitted to Spotlight. Remember that topic we created back at the beginning of the book? Try searching for that now. Type in "snapchatbook" and then tap on the topic. You'll see a collection of Snaps from everyone who sent one in. Check it out!

STORIES

On the Stories page, accessible as the fourth item over on the main action bar, you'll find posted Snaps from your friends, posts from accounts that you subscribe to, and professionally produced short-form content especially made for Snapchat.

FRIENDS AND GROUP STORIES

At the top of the list are posts that your Snapchat friends have pushed to their My Story. These posts will remain viewable for 24 hours from when they were posted. And unlike a direct Snap, you can rewatch these posts as long as they're active. This section also includes Group Stories posts.

General Info: *Group Stories*

Much like Group Chats, Group Stories are a common story shared among Snapchat friends. Anyone in the group can post to it and see the stories contributed to it.

Subscriptions

Under the Subscriptions section are Snaps that are created by people you subscribe to who have posted to their Public Story. These accounts can be from verified accounts like Celebrities, Influencers, Lens Creators, or Brands, and they can also be from anyone who has a public profile set up and has posted to that Story.

Discover

Discover features a variety of content that Snapchat thinks you might be interested in, from professionally produced entertainment and news to trending Influencer stories to Bitmoji stories to Snapchat Originals, which are exclusive to the Snapchat platform.

In the final spot on the action bar, Spotlight is Snapchat's answer to the wildly popular social media platform TikTok. It features the best short videos from across the Snapchat platform. If you're the kind of person who can spend hours on TikTok, swiping for that next video, this is definitely the spot for you. Tap the Trending button in the upper right corner to see the current trending topics. And if you're looking for videos of something in particular, use Search to find the topic of choice.

General Info: *Spotlight Payouts*

To incentivize people to contribute to Spotlight, Snap is giving away cash prizes every day to the creators with the top "favorited" posts. If your TikTok game is strong, it never hurts to give Snapchat Spotlight a shot as well.

PROFILE AND SETTINGS

An easily overlooked, but critical, part of your Snapchat experience is your User Profile. For some people, it can be a "set it and forget it" kind of thing. Much of this is configured when you sign up for an account in the first place. But for me, the profile screen is my window to my fans and the people who follow my story. I'm constantly visiting my profile page for insights into the stories and Lenses that I create. The user profile is the gateway to important analytics and information about your account. Plus, Snapchat just released a pretty significant Bitmoji-focused update to the profile screen, with some fun new changes there. Let's examine the user profile page so you can make sure it's working best for how you use Snapchat.

A. Bitmoji Customization
B. Share Profile
C. User Snapcode
D. Display and Username
C. Snap Score and Sun Sign
D. Public Profiles
E. Stories
F. Spotlight and Snap Map
G. Friends
H. Snap Map
I. Settings

Bitmoji Customization

In a big change from previous iterations of the app, Snapchat is now making your Bitmoji a big part of your profile. Assuming your Bitmoji is already set up, this is where you can edit and customize it. There are almost endless possibilities for the way you can make your Bitmoji look. There's no rule that says your Bitmoji has to look exactly like you, either. You want a

purple mullet and muttonchops beard? Go for it.

Hit the Hanger button to quickly change outfits—if you're a fashionista, don't worry, there's new looks, brand names, and even seasonal outfits on display. You can also edit your Bitmoji itself. And the great thing is that whatever you change on your Bitmoji gets updated across all of Snapchat, including stickers and any AR Lenses and filters that use it.

With the Image button on the other side, you can also change your Bitmoji's Pose and Background. Scroll through a wide variety of different colorful options and make your Bitmoji's pose match your attitude.

Notable Feature: *Bitmoji Keyboard*

Did you know that you can send Bitmoji stickers to people from apps outside of Snapchat, like text messaging or iMessage? From the Bitmoji app, select the Keyboard button on the bottom, then tap "Turn on Keyboard" to enable it. You'll have access to the Bitmoji sticker library right from your keyboard in whatever app you're in that uses the system keyboard.

Share Profile

The way you share your profile just got a lot snazzier. Before this latest update, sharing your profile meant sending out a regular URL link, but now your well-dressed Bitmoji becomes your calling card—ready to invite a friendship connection through Snapchat, Instagram/Facebook, Messenger, or anywhere you care to post the link.

User Snapcode

You may be familiar with QR (Quick Response) codes, which allow a camera on a smartphone to scan a unique visual tag and have it open a link to a webpage. The Snap Code is that same concept, except it is a link to you—or at least your Snapchat account. If someone scans that code, they'll be prompted to add you on Snapchat. Tapping on this will bring up a larger view of the Snapcode that a friend can scan. You'll also get a few other options, including downloading a digital image of your Snapcode, which you could use on a website, email signature, or even printed on a business card. There's an option to share your Snapcode as a URL, so you could text it to a friend.

Display Name

This is the name that most people will see if you post something or message them in the Chat. You can easily change your username by tapping on it.

Username

Your username was set up when you created your account. Due to security reasons, Snap does not allow you to change it, except in extremely rare circumstances.

Snap Score

A user's Snap Score is based on their usage of Snapchat. Sending and receiving Snaps, Chats, Streaks, and Stickers to your fellow Snapchat users raises your score. So, just because there's a score, does it mean that this is a competition, with leaderboards and prizes for the most points? No. The points don't actually matter. There's no need to freak out if you have a low score. And it's also not necessary to try to raise your score. (Trust me, there's videos on YouTube that will teach you how.) A low score just means you have a new account or haven't used Snapchat as much. The real winners on Snapchat are those who have quality interactions with each other.

Sun Sign

For those of you who are into astrology, your sun sign, based on the birthdate you provided, will be displayed here. Not much else to mention here, other than that your sign will come back into play when we discuss Friendship Profiles.

General Info: *Tips and News*

Occasionally Snapchat will send you notifications and tips on ho
to better utilize the app. That information will show up here on yo
profile screen. It could be recommendations for completing your
profile, tips on how Spotlight works, or other helpful pointers for having a good in-app experience. And from time to time, you may also
receive public service information about important events, like how
to register to vote.

is section will give you a quick overview of what's going on with your osts to that story. We'll discuss Public Profiles in greater depth in a later hapter, but here are a few key features of interest:

General Info: *Creator Profile-Only Features*

Some of the features listed in this section are not available for a standard Public Profile. They are only available to Creator/Business Profiles. See the Public vs. Creator Profile section for more information on this. Regular Public Profiles will only show you

A. Public Story thumbnail view: This is what your public profile thumbnail looks like. Tap on it to see your public story posts.
B. Total views: The total number of people who have viewed your story.
C. Total Story replies: The total number of replies to your posts.
D. Post thumbnail: Thumbnail of an individual post. Tap on it to see that post.
E. Text block and post time: The last block of text used on a post will appear here, along with a notation of how long ago it was posted.
F. Share: This button provides a link that allows you to share a post outside Snapchat, whether it be a text, Twitter, or Facebook.
G. Post views and replies: The views and story replies to an individual post.
H. Access Public Profile menu: Tap this to access your public profile menu.

Stories

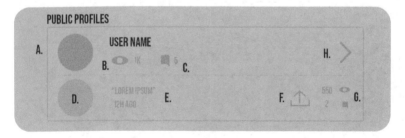

Snaps posted to your story will be listed here, along with view counts. Depending on your privacy settings, your personal story will only be visible to your friends. You can even customize it further so that only certain friends can view it. You can also tap "New Story" and create a separate custom story visible only to the friends you choose.

Spotlight and Snap Map

Snaps that you post to Spotlight are listed here, along with their view counts. Spotlight posts are public and are also accessible on the Snap Map. Under "My Spotlight Favorites," you'll find a history of any Spotlight videos that you gave a heart to.

Friends

This section gives you a quick look at your top closest friends on Snapchat. Under this section, you'll also find the Add Friends submenu, pending friend requests, and your contact list in Snapchat. Tapping on one of your friends' Bitmojis will bring up your friendship profile with them.

Snap Map

This is your quick view of your Snap Map. You can easily change your Bitmoji's outfit or activity here. Or tap on the map itself to access all its features.

General Info: *Snapchat Start Date*

At the very bottom of your profile page is the date when you joined Snapchat.

Settings

The settings menu contains all the details of your account information. Most of the things here you can change by tapping on them, the major exception being your username. There's a few things under the settings menu that I'd like to point out in order for you to have a full mastery of your Snapchat account.

Birthday

Under the Birthday item, there's a slider called Birthday Party. With it enabled, Snapchat will add a birthday-cake charm next to your name in the Contacts list on your friends' accounts—just to let them know to wish you a happy birthday. If you don't want them to know when your birthday is, just disable this feature.

Mobile Number/Email

If your phone number changes or you change email accounts, you'll definitely want to update that information here as soon as possible. It keeps your account more secure; and if you allow yourself to be search-able by that information, it lets friends find you that way as well.

Password

A strong password is your first step in keeping your account secure. Snapchat requires that you choose a password that is at least 8 char-acters long and that uses a combination of uppercase and lowercase letters as well as numbers and symbols. Also, it should go without say-ing that you should never share your password with anyone else, that you don't reuse your password from another account, and that you don't use personal information in your password like birthday, name, address, phone number, or the word "password."

If you suspect that you've been hacked, reset your password right away. And if you can't reset it, or you've been locked out, contact Snap immedi-ately on their support website: Support.Snapchat.com

Two-Factor Authentication (2FA)

Two-Factor Authentication is an important additional safeguard for your ac-count. It requires a secondary login step for someone trying to gain access to your account. This can be done with either an SMS message sent to your phone or an authenticator app such as Google Authenticator or Duo Security app. You can specify here in settings whether you'd like to receive an SMS, Authentication code, or both. With Two-Factor authentication, even if some-one hacks your password, Snapchat can send a text with your temporary

2FA code to your phone—and without that code, the hacker won't be able to get access to your account.

So if you haven't done so already, be sure and set up your 2FA.

Pro Tip: Recover Code

As an additional backup to two-factor authentication, you can set up a re-covery code as well in case you are unable to receive an SMS and/or can't use the Authenticator app. This is basically an additional password that you will enter when you log in. And definitely keep this code in a safe place—Snapchat can't help you with a lost recovery code.

Pro Tip: *Linked Devices*

If you've changed or upgraded your phone, it may still be listed as a verified device in Snapchat. It's easy to remove it. Just tap on Two-Factor Authentication and go to Forget Devices. You'll see a list of which devices are authorized for your account. Tap the X on the right to make Snapchat forget that old device. Also, it never hurts to go in here once in a while and double-check to make sure you recognize all the devices that are authorized to your Snapchat account.

Notifications

While our smartphones are great at keeping us up-to-the-minute with every-thing going on in the world, they can actually be very disruptive to our attention and focus. It's good to both set aside some time away from these distractions entirely, and to also pare down the amount of distractions you receive on a daily basis. Under your phone's Notification settings, you can turn off all notifications from Snapchat—but with this menu, you can actually select the specific types of notifications you do receive. Under the Notifications tab inside of Snapchat, there are sliders limiting which types of content you will receive notifications about. So, if you want Snapchat to let you know if you're mentioned in someone's story or get to see when it's a friend's birthday, you can easily customize that here.

Stories I Follow

In the early days after I was verified, I started posting a lot of stories to my account. Some would say "an *obnoxious* amount." And in all honesty, they wouldn't be wrong. The problem that some people ran into was that they would be receiving pings every time I posted. So let's just say hypothetically that if I posted 90 times to my story in a single day, I would have certainly worn out my welcome to a few of my friends and put myself dangerously close to being considered a social-media war criminal. I do remember having a few people asking me to stop. If only they had known that Snapchat also allows you to turn off notifications to a particular story if it's becoming a bit much.

At the bottom of the Notifications screen is the Manage Story Notifications tab. Under it, you can find a person's name and turn on (or off) the notifications of their particular story. You still remain friends (or subscribers) and get to follow their content on your own terms.

And on a personal note, I've learned to be much more selective about the quality and quantity of what I post.

Memories

If you remember back to the section on saving Snaps, this menu item lets you decide what happens when you hit that Save button. Here you can decide the destination of a saved Snap—whether it goes to Snapchat's servers as a Memory or to the Camera Roll using your device's internal storage—or both.

If you're more conscious of saving your data on your phone plan, you can also change when those Snaps get backed up—using Wi-Fi only, or allowing Snapchat to use your data if Wi-Fi is unavailable.

And if your content quality is gold medal every single time and you want to save every Snap you create, there's an option here for that as well.

Flashbacks

One final feature here is whether or not you want to receive Flashbacks. These are little photo/video montages of Snaps that you've saved, which Snapchat creates for you. I personally like seeing back to the Snaps I took on my beach vacation last year; but, like any non-essential software feature, sometimes it's nice to be able to turn it off.

Spectacles

Snap Inc. is not only behind the Snapchat app, but they've also been steadily iterating on the stylish and functional sunglasses with built-in cameras called Spectacles. These were designed specifically to work with Snapchat for capturing first-person moments. The first two versions had a single camera, and Spectacles 3 has two cameras which can record footage in 3D. The latest version of Spectacles takes another leap forward and can actually display augmented reality effects inside the glasses. I highly recommend you go to Spectacles.com to see footage of them in action. They're very cool.

If you are the owner of a pair of Spectacles, here is where you can manage their connection to Snapchat. And if you don't own a pair, there's a Shop button where you can order them.

On-Demand Geofilters

If you've created any Geofilters with your snapchat account, you'll find a list of them here. See the section on Geofilters to learn how to create them.

Shazam

As mentioned earlier, Snapchat's music scan is integrated with Shazam to search for a song. So if you have used this feature to scan for music, you'll find a list of all those results here.

Payments and Snap Store

These work together to allow you to purchase items from Snapchat. Payments stores your credit card information and Snap Store sells Snapchat-related merchandise, including items printed with your Bitmoji and Snap Spectacles.

Snap Codes

This is a record of all the snap codes you've scanned. You can quickly scroll through the list and reactivate a code you've scanned. There's also an option to scan a snap code from a photo you've taken.

Partner Connections

This is a list of any other apps with an integration to Snapchat that you've allowed to access your Snapchat information. It's good to occasionally check this list and make sure only apps that you're still using have access.

Voice Scan

This is where you can activate the voice-scan feature for Lens Explorer. Please note that voice scan only works in Lens Explorer, not as a regular screen scan.

App Appearance

Finally, and after years of public outcry, here is where you can activate Dark Mode in Snapchat. Now Snapchat's Twitter followers can find something else to complain about—or go back to whining about being unable to change usernames.

Friendship Profiles

Each friend you have on Snapchat will have a Friendship Profile accessible by tapping on their profile image. This shares many similarities with your own Profile, including the Bitmoji-centric design, but with a few key differences. Here's what it looks like:

A. Friend's Bitmoji
B. Display Name
C. Chat and Call Buttons
D. Public Profile (Optional)
E. Snap Map
F. Saved in Chat
G. Chat Attachments
H. Charms
I. Profile Options

Friend's Bitmoji

Here we have your friend's Bitmoji on display, set up according to their preferences for pose, clothing style, and background. You do not have the option to change anything about your friend's Bitmoji.

Chat/Call Buttons

These are quick-access buttons to start a conversation or a call with the owner of the Friendship Profile.

Tips

Highlights information specific to Friendship Profiles; for instance, if you screenshot a Friendship Profile, the other person will be notified about that.

Public Profile

If your friend has a Public Profile, you can access their profile page here.

Snap Map

Displays your friend's location on the Snap Map—if they've shared that with you. If not, you can request it and also share your own location.

Saved In Chat

This is a list of any images or videos that you've saved in the chat.

Chat Attachments

Any saved links that you've shared with your friend, including Lens links.

Charms

Charms are little badges that Snap gives you for things like being in touch, best friends, sun sign compatibility, combined Snap score average, and even one for it being their birthday.

Profile Options

This might be the most useful part of a friendship profile. Here's where you can change when Snaps delete in the chat (it defaults to immediately, but I like to change it to 24 hours). You can also clear the conversation, pin the conversation (which keeps their profile pinned to the top of your chat screen for easy access), change if you get notified when they send you a message, and even share their profile with another Snapchat friend.

There's also safety options here to Report, Block, and Remove Friends for those people who are misbehaving. It's unfortunate to have to use those options, but they are important for protecting yourself on social media.

Public Profile

For those who are interested in using Snapchat to build an audience, a Public Profile is a must. Whether you're someone just getting started in the social-media game, a public figure, a business, or a brand, your Public Profile on Snapchat is a good way to gain and communicate with your audience. While the term "influencer" has taken a tarnish in recent years, there's no reason why you can't use the Snapchat platform to thoughtfully communicate with a larger group of people who care what you have to say. That all starts with a Public Profile.

Much in the same way that we don't all really need our own personal website, the average Snapchat user does not need to set up a public profile. This section is really for people, brands, and businesses who are trying to communicate with their followers on Snapchat—who want to use the extra features designed for audience communication, insight, and growth. If that's not you, feel free to skip this section.

To get your Public Profile set up, tap the three dots beside "Add to Snap Map" on your Profile page and tap "Create Public Profile." Snapchat will then guide you through the process. And if you do create a public profile and would like to delete it, you can do that under the Profile menu, selecting My Public Profile, then Settings, and finally Delete.

PUBLIC PROFILE VS CREATOR/BUSINESS PROFILE

I wanted to pause for a brief moment to make an important distinction on profiles. A Public Profile that you set up on your own will give you some great features for reaching an audience. A Public Profile will give you:

- Public Profile Page with your Photo, Bio, Description, Location, Highlights, and Snapchat Lenses
- Subscription button that allows users to subscribe to you
- Subscriber count

A Creator or Business Profile (also known as a verified account) has all the above features, plus:

- Story, Lens, and Audience Insights
- A Public Story separate from My Story
- Ability to add a website and email to your Profile Page
- A category for your public profile
- A Chat button on your public profile (if you activate it in your privacy settings)
- Snapchatters can turn on Story Notifications for you
- Assign and Manage roles on your profile
- Enable Story Replies and Quoting

It's important to note that as I discuss Public Profiles, the examples I use will be for all the features available for a Creator/Business Profile. I wanted to include, for the most people possible, as much helpful information as I could in this book, without repeating myself on overlapping features. So if you've created a standard Public Profile on your own and are like "Hey, I don't have story replies, management roles, or audience analytics on my profile," that's because your Public Profile account type doesn't have those features. But it is possible to get a Creator profile. If you start with a Public Profile and gain a hundred subscribers, Snap may provide you with a Creator account.

Let's look at the Public Profile screen and see what features it has to offer:

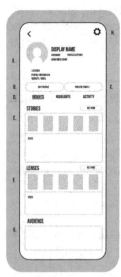

A. Profile Information
B. Edit Profile
C. Preview Profile
D. Insights/Highlights/Activity
E. Stories
F. Lenses
G. Audience
H. Settings

Profile Information

Like your personal profile, the Public Profile will also contain information like Display Name and Username. In addition, it will also show what Public Profile category you belong to, your location, your profile description, your website, and even your subscriber count.

Edit Profile

This is where you set up all the information in your Public Profile, including your profile picture. And you have the option to choose whether you want to display your subscriber count. Anything you don't want visible to the public, don't include it here.

General Info: *Profile Categories*

When you are setting up your profile, you'll be asked to select a category for what type of public profile you are creating. They have a lot to choose from—too many to mention here. So whether you're an individual, business, or brand, make sure you choose the one that most accurately represents you.

Preview Profile

This allows you to see what the public sees when they're looking at your public profile page. It will give you a good picture of how you're representing yourself. Does that profile picture accurately reflect who you are? Are your recent highlights "on brand" with your image? Here's where you can get the best sense of how the public is seeing you.

Insights/Highlights/Activity

Of the three pages nested in these tabs, you'll be using the Insights way more than the others. Insights provides analytics on Story and Snapchat Lens performance, as well as audience demographics and interest. These are helpful for understanding what your audience is responding to and what wasn't a hit. Highlights lets you quickly add or remove the Highlights on your profile. Activity is a log of what was posted to your Public Story account— which really comes into play when you have more than one person posting to a Public Story account (for business or brand accounts, for example).

Stories

This gives you a quick overview of your daily Story postings. At a glance you can see how many posts you've made, a thumbnail of the latest one, and, for previous days, a rough total of views. Directly below this is a 28-day summary of the performance metrics of your Stories, like amount of views, number of viewers, and average view time. You'll also get a comparison percent change versus the previous 28 days. Tap on the "See All Stories" button to go back to any Story you've ever created. You'll also be able to see a day-to-day breakdown of views over time.

Lenses

Here is a list of all the Snapchat Lenses uploaded to your account, starting with your most recent. And just like Stories, you also get a 28-day summary of metrics for how your Lenses have performed overall and a percent change versus the previous time frame. These metrics include views, reach, shares, plays, Snap Camera Play Time, and Snap Camera Total View Time. Tapping on See All Lenses will show you all your Lenses along with views for each, and a day-by-day breakdown of views. Tap on a Lens here and select View Insights for the performance statistics of an individual Lens.

Audience

The Audience section lets you know how many current subscribers you have and percentage change versus the past 28 days. It also gives you a basic breakdown of your audience—Men %, Women %, Location, and Top Interest. Going into the See More for this category will give you a much more in-depth view of your audience, breakdown by gender and age group, Top 5 Locations, and Top 5 Interests. This can be really helpful as you plan out your posts. Knowing your audience will help you better speak to them about the things that matter to them.

Settings

The options for Settings for your Public Profile are a lot different from what you'll find under your Personal Profile. Here it's all about how you want to manage your profile. You can add roles to another Snapchat user to either be an admin, collaborator, Story contributor, or Insight viewer to your Public Profile. You'll be able to select if you want to view Story replies, add muted words, add Story attributions (if you have added Story contributors or collaborators), and get notified if one of your contributors posted on your Story.

General Info: *Muted words*

An unfortunate part about being a public figure on the Internet is the possibility of receiving unwanted, abusive, or rude messages from random people. Muted words are a list of words (symbols, abbreviations, or any combination thereof) that you can have Snapchat use to flag and filter out messages from people you don't want to receive. For example, if you hate laser tag and don't want to talk about it, you can enter those words in your muted words list, and none of those messages with either of those words will appear in your story replies.

Story Insights

With a Public Profile, viewers of your story can swipe up on a post and send you a message in reply. These are viewable when you tap on the Views/Replies button for an individual post. That screen looks like this:

A. Story Posts Overview
B. Post Views and Replies
C. Insights
D. Story Replies
E. Reply Response Sticker
F. Viewers List

Story Posts Overview

This is a list of all your posts for the past day, starting with your most recent. Any text block you added to the post will become its title at the top. You can scroll back through the posts and tap on an individual one to review it.

Post Views and Replies

With each post is a count of views and replies to it. Story replies for that post will be displayed down below the Insights block.

Insights

Here is your overall public story performance metrics. Included are how many total views by subscribers and non-subscribers alike, as well as total screenshots of your posts and total Story replies.

Story Replies

Story replies allow your followers to respond to your individual posts by swiping up on them and sending you a message. All those messages appear here. You'll see the display name of the person who sent the message, the message itself, and how long ago they sent it. You have the option to tap on the message and reply directly to them if you wish. Don't forget that you can turn off Story replies under your Public Profile settings, and you can use the word filter to make sure you don't get messages with certain words in them.

Reply Response Sticker

I love this feature a lot. With it, you can turn someone's comment into a sticker on a Snap, so you can reply directly to them on your story for everyone to see. They'll also get a direct message of the post as well. It's a fun way to get feedback from your fans and include them in your story—which I've found to be quite popular.

Viewers List

If you're curious about who actually viewed your story, look no further. The viewers list is everyone, friend or other, who checked out a post.

Public Profile Summary

A Snapchat Public Profile is a great way to extend your reach to an audience. It helps you engage with the millions of Snapchat users around the world and, because your content is fresh and also temporary, it encourages your fans to check in with you more frequently. Showing the fun and cool moments from your everyday life will also give people a better glimpse into your world and let them know who you are as a person. But I also want to point out that a Snapchat Public Profile won't replace all your other social media channels. It's good to "cross-pollinate" your content across other platforms, giving your work the best chance to reach the most people.

SNAP SAFETY

Snapchat is an awesome place to communicate and be creative. It should also be a safe place where you can be yourself. However, to paraphrase the character Alfred from the movie *The Dark Knight*, "Some people just want to watch the world burn." Whether it's just a kid trying to be "edgy," someone's having a bad day, or they're just a straight-up unrepentant jerk, we can't control the actions of other people, and there's a possibility that you may encounter one of these people on Snapchat. Fortunately, the folks at Snap take online safety seriously and you have a few available options if you do encounter one of these uncool humans. Here's a few tips to help you have a good experience on Snapchat.

Privacy

As a general rule on the Internet, it's good to protect what data you're putting out there. Every person has their own comfort level with what that is exactly, but it's good to ask yourself the question and make sure you are comfortable with what you're allowing to be available. That's why Snap recommends that you review the "Who can. . ." section of Settings to make sure the settings there reflect your privacy preferences.

Unwelcome Behavior on Snapchat

No one wants to be bullied, receive unwanted messages, or be harassed in other ways on social media. It's important to remember how to Block, Report, and Unfriend someone who is behaving badly. Just tap on their profile and then the three dots in the upper right corner. That will bring up the menu where you can remove them from your Snapchat experience. Even if the behavior is not worthy of reporting, you don't have to put up with people who are stressing you out or acting in a toxic way, but you should definitely report violations to Snapchat's terms of service.

Well-Being

Something that I really respect about Snapchat is their push to not just be a platform where you can share moments with people, but that they actually do care about the Snapchatter's personal welfare. They've included a

Here For You tool to provide resources from localized organizations when you search for words associated with being in crisis. From anxiety, bullying, LGBTQ identity, mental health, and more, Snapchat will provide you with connections and resources ready to help. And not just for yourself, either: Snapchat has reporting tools for alerting if you're worried about a friend who is at risk for self-harm.

Snapchat has also partnered with Crisis Text Line to connect its users with trained counselors, ready to help those in need. They are ready to listen and help with issues like anxiety, depression, self-harm, eating disorders, suicide prevention, and more.

Even if you're not in crisis, Snapchat has tools for general maintenance of mental well-being. With the Headspace mini, you can take a few moments to refocus and recenter yourself with breathing exercises and meditation. Or use it to check in with your friends—remember that they might need a little encouragement, too.

SUMMARY AND CONCLUSION

As someone who picked up Snapchat late in the game, it was a bit intimidating to me. I often struggled with knowing where everything was and what it did. So it took me a while before I was really comfortable using the app. And even now, I think there's still things within Snapchat that I could know more about and be better at. But I hope, as you complete this book, that you have not only the confidence that you can create and share Snaps that capture the important moments in your life, but the confidence that you have a more complete understanding of Snapchat than some people who have been using the app for years.

The real value in Snapchat is to be able to use it to improve the way you share what matters with those who are important to you. I specifically avoided telling you what to Snap, because that will be different for everyone. How you choose to use Snapchat is up to you. My hope is that with the information you've gleaned from this book, you'll be able to make Snapchat an integral part of how you connect with friends, reach an audience, and use your own creativity to make the world a better place—in whatever way that means to you.

ACKNOWLEDGMENTS

I want to thank everyone who supported me along the way to completing this book. First and foremost, a huge THANK YOU to Snap, Inc. for creating this wonderful app and all the awesome people there who have encouraged and advised me with this endeavor, specifically Kaitlyn Benitez-Strine. Thanks also to everyone else who helped me through the writing process: Kyle Holloway, Cyrene Quiamco, Pam Taylor, Dustin Ballard, Tiffani Sahara, Sallia Goldstein, Carey Nelson-Burch, and Marisa Munoz. Finally thank you to my family, who finds it curious that I make a living creating augmented reality potatoes and other such nonsense, but loves me anyway.

While his Potato Snapchat Lens gets all the glory, Phil Walton has spent years working in storytelling and creative 3D art. After serving in the Air Force, Phil returned to school to study animation and, after ten years as a 3D character animator, found new opportunities in the realm of Augmented Reality. His distinctive Snapchat Lenses have been viewed around the world over 4.5 billion times, and have appeared on the Super Bowl pregame show, *Saturday Night Live*, *The Late Late Show with James Corden*, *The Late Show with Jimmy Kimmel*, music videos, viral tweets, *Twitch Streams*, and countless TikToks. Phil is also the lead AR developer, creating the unique augmented reality characters, on the TV show Nickelodeon's *Unfiltered*. He lives in Tennessee and can be found at his various social media channels.

Snapchat @phillip.walton
Instagram @phillip.walton
Twitter @fireandknife
Phillipwalton.com